Wealth-Building

Journal

BLACK ENTERPRISE

Wealth - Building Journal

A DAY-BY-DAY JOURNEY TO A BRIGHTER FUTURE, A BETTER YOU

THE EDITORS OF BLACK ENTERPRISE MAGAZINE

John Wiley & Sons, Inc.

ISBN 0-471-07909-X

Printed in the United States of America.

10 9 8 7 6 5 4 3 2 1

Contents

Introduction   *1*

Black Enterprise Declaration of Financial Empowerment   *3*

CHAPTER 1: Getting Started   *5*

CHAPTER 2: Saving Your Money   *27*

CHAPTER 3: Managing Debt and Credit   *49*

CHAPTER 4: Being a Smart Consumer   *63*

CHAPTER 5: Getting into the Game of Investing   *83*

CHAPTER 6: Your Midyear Assessment   *105*

CHAPTER 7: Handling Your Taxes   *119*

CHAPTER 8: Maximizing Your Earning Potential   *137*

CHAPTER 9: Helping to Strengthen Your Community   *157*

CHAPTER 10: Teaching Your Children Well   *175*

CHAPTER 11: Passing on Wealth to Future Generations   *189*

CHAPTER 12: Your Annual Review   *203*

Resources   *215*

Introduction

In 1995, the *Black Enterprise* Board of Economists met to discuss what to do about the wealth gap between African Americans and whites in the United States. They brainstormed together, focusing on the unrealized financial potential of our community and the need for a strategy, a "new deal," to achieve true economic parity. Out of this exciting meeting the *Black Enterprise* Wealth-Building Initiative was born. The initiative is a call to arms for African Americans to take our finances into our own hands and realize our own vision of the American dream.

At *Black Enterprise,* we have made it our mission for the twenty-first century to provide you with the tools essential to making your aspirations come true. This is a program for *everyone,* from those who are really struggling to the very well off. Regardless of your level of education, experience, or income, you can gain from making a renewed commitment to building wealth. A desire to strengthen the sense of community among African Americans is what truly drives this mission. We hope to build a financially healthier, more ambitious, and more influential community one person at a time, one day at a time.

The centerpiece of the Black Wealth-Building Initiative is the Declaration of Financial Empowerment, a self-empowerment tool for those who are committed to embracing real change in their lifestyles. We ask you to start this process by reading the declaration, reflecting on it, and, finally, signing on and *committing to it.* Take the challenge of adopting our principles of wealth creation, and design the life that you and your family so richly deserve.

Central to the Declaration of Financial Empowerment is what we call the Circle of Wealth. The circle begins with the knowledge and understanding of what you need and *can* do to build personal wealth. The second step is to make a lasting commitment to change and growth, followed by investing. Yes, we mean investing your dollars in the capital markets, but also investing *yourself* in the pursuit of financial awareness and health. It is our hope that you will all become avid readers of the financial pages, that you will keep a keen eye on your progress, and that you will see a marked difference in your behavior as a consumer. Over time you will have your own portfolio to manage, which will materialize in your goal of wealth accumulation. Finally, we urge you to commit to reinvesting your wealth in your family, in future generations, and back into the African American community. You will find that financial empowerment affects many aspects of your life that you might not expect—from your career to raising your children.

This journal is designed to help you stick with it, to be a guide and a companion along your year-long wealth-building journey. Your year begins right now, whether it is January, May, or December. We also hope this year will be just the first of many years in which you keep a financial journal, a record of your progress and state of mind as you work hard to build wealth and security. "Like it or not," warns Earl G. Graves, publisher of *Black Enterprise,* "in this society it's always about money and the leverage of economic power for the greatest power: the freedom to live as you want to live." This freedom is what we want you to achieve for yourself and future generations. "I would hope that five years from now," Graves says, "when someone asks how this program started, it will be said that we were the drum majors for something that was very critical to the black community."

Be a part of this movement. Turn the page, commit, and begin your journey today.

Black Enterprise Declaration of Financial Empowerment

Today Is the Day I Take Control of My Financial Destiny

In order to attain a measure of success, power, and wealth, I shall uphold the principles of saving and investing as well as controlled spending and disciplined consumerism. I vow to fully participate in the capital markets and make a solid commitment to a program of wealth accumulation. Determination and consistency will serve as my guides, and I will not and cannot allow external or internal forces to keep me from reaching my goals. By adjusting my course and embracing a new mandate that stresses planning, education, and fortitude, I lay a strong, unbreakable foundation for the preservation and enrichment of my family, children, and children's children.

I, _____,
from this day forward, declare my vigilant and lifelong commitment to financial empowerment. I pledge the following:

1. To save and invest 10 to 15 percent of my after-tax income

2. To be a proactive and informed investor

3. To be a disciplined and knowledgeable consumer

4. To measure my personal wealth by net worth, not income

5. To engage in sound budget, credit, and tax management practices

6. To teach business and financial practices to my children

7. To use a portion of my personal wealth to strengthen my community

8. To support the creation and growth of profitable, competitive black-owned enterprises

9. To maximize my earning power through a commitment to career development, technological literacy, and professional excellence

10. To ensure that my wealth is passed on to future generations

I have committed to this unwavering, personal covenant as a means of bolstering myself, my family, and my community. In adopting this resolution, I intend to use all available resources, wisdom, and power to gain my share of the American dream.

Agreed and Signed: _____ Date: _____

Getting Started

The legendary Reginald F. Lewis, the first African American to create a billion-dollar business, paved a path for countless other businesspeople by breaking seemingly impossible racial barriers on Wall Street. At the time of his early death from brain cancer at the age of 50, his worth was estimated by *Forbes* magazine at $400 million, and he was placed on their list of the 400 wealthiest Americans.

A lawyer, entrepreneur, and philanthropist, Lewis built his empire from scratch. He was a persevering kid from a working-class neighborhood in Baltimore, who started earning money at the age of 10. In high school he worked nights in a drugstore after football practice and as a waiter at a country club on the weekends. While at Virginia State College he was a night manager for a bowling alley and a salesman for a photography company. All the while, Lewis aggressively pursued his true professional goals.

He reached an important milestone in his life when he was accepted to Harvard Law School and, as it was with so many of his other accomplishments, he found the exceptional motivation to follow through. After attending a summer program for minorities at the law school, he was told politely by the administration that if he wanted to become a lawyer, they would recommend him to other law schools around the country. Lewis didn't settle for that answer. Instead, he persisted, pleading his case and winning the support of key figures who helped turn his situation around. In his book *Why Should White Guys Have All the Fun? How Reginald Lewis Created a Billion-Dollar Business Empire,* Lewis described a conversation he had with his college roommate before attending the summer program: "The letter came. I was going to Harvard for the summer. I told my roommate, 'Come September, I will be in the incoming class at Harvard Law.' He said, 'Reg, this is just for the summer. Don't set yourself up for a major disappointment.' I said, 'Just watch, I'm going to Harvard.' "

Are some people simply more motivated to be financially successful than other people? When you read about Reginald Lewis, do you recall your own drive early on to make money and your resolve to take all the necessary steps, or do you think: "I could never be like that. I wouldn't even know where to begin"?

This first chapter is about getting started, about taking the initiative to begin your own personal journey to financial empowerment. We may not all end up as icons like Lewis, but *each of us,* regardless of our current situation, has the potential to reach clear financial goals and overcome obstacles along the way. As you make your way through these first four weeks, remember that your primary task is to get motivated.

What is motivation, really? The dictionary defines *motive* as simply "something (a need or desire) that causes a person to act." The word can also mean a recurrent phrase or figure that is developed with use. If we think of our own dreams as *motifs,* they may end up being actualized differently than they were initially imagined. Experts in the field of psychology advise parents to give a child a dream; let the child hope to become an inventor, an Olympic athlete, or a famous actor. Even if the child falls short of the dream, it will certainly have made the child more successful overall. Every person must start out with an idea of what his or her goal or dream is.

Develop your own personal goal—knowing it may change— that you will carry throughout all 12 months, all tasks and stages, of this journal. Your motivator could be that at the end of the year you will have enough money to lease that car you've been dreaming about. It could be that you want to get as far out of debt as you can and start the next year with a clean slate. It could be that you will establish a college savings plan for your grandchild or that you will finally have the equity to begin thinking about starting your own business.

Just as you declared that this is the day you make the change to become financially empowered, believe that this is the *year* that you will change your personal finances forever. You will have long-term goals that may not be met by the end of this year, but, most important, you will have a firm foundation on which to build.

Establish your goals—one for the end of this year and a longer-term goal. Assign a deadline for the latter.

_____

_____

_____

_____

_____

_____

_____

_____

_____

_____

_____

_____

_____

Throughout his life, Lewis displayed exceptional initiative and industry. In order to learn how to take initiative and become more industrious, it's helpful to understand the barriers that keep most people from working diligently toward a goal or from even getting started. Contemporary theories in psychology contend that worry or guilt can get in the way of devising and implementing a plan. If guilty emotions are not acknowledged and addressed, they can create a cycle that leads to inertia. Sounds like psychobabble, but it's a common real-life problem.

For example, two hardworking parents of a girl who is academically gifted worry that they will not be able to save enough money to send their daughter to the best private college of her choice. That very guilt and worry may actually be what keeps them from taking the first step to achieving a viable savings plan.

A single professional finds himself spending money on entertainment and luxury items that his parents, who were extremely frugal when he was growing up, would have never even considered. Lots of money is coming in, but it goes out just as quickly, and he can't seem to get a handle on his spending or get himself to open that 401(k) account. Perhaps he is trying to make up for all he experienced as being withheld from him as a kid. But once the money is spent, he frets about his spending habits—so much so that his only option is denial of his financial well being. Being bogged down by guilt is one of the primary things that keep people from taking control of their financial lives.

Can you think of what issues along these lines might be standing in your way? As you write them down, release them. Then move on, allowing yourself a fresh start.

_____

_____

_____

_____

_____

_____

Other emotional issues that keep one inactive are lack of confidence and fear of failure. We hear a lot about the importance of self-esteem these days; feelings of inferiority do create a tendency for us to withdraw from challenging situations. The safest way not to fail is not to try. It is also the safest way not to succeed or grow. Negative attitudes about pursuing wealth can have their origins in unexpected places. They don't have to relate directly to your financial or even professional life.

How do you see your financial life so far? Consider creating an image or a story like the preceding one about Reginald Lewis that you might hope people will tell about you someday.

_____

_____

_____

_____

_____

_____

_____

_____

_____

_____

_____

_____

_____

Having touched on the emotional side of getting started, let's move on to the intellectual side. This is not about assessing your knowledge of statistics or financial history. It's about knowing your own cognitive style, the different ways in which you go about accomplishing both the simplest and most complex tasks. Just as there are two sides of the brain, there are, generally, two cognitive styles. Most of us don't fall neatly into one category or the other, but rather somewhere along a continuum between the two.

One style of thinking is analytical, careful, and logical. Such a person is thoughtful, organized, and often systematic in the way he or she goes about completing tasks. The other is more impulsive, rapid, and intuitive, rendering the person highly creative and more apt to make insightful associations.

For example, you may not be good at organizing and recoil at the thought of a spreadsheet, but you are an exceptionally creative person, with talents those around you envy. Therefore, sitting down to complete some of the worksheets in the pages ahead could take two or three attempts, but you might also discover that you have a gift for picking stocks. Conversely, maybe you get real comfort from the satisfaction of knowing that every dollar you spend is carefully accounted for in your monthly budget, which you always meet or go under, but if you're not careful, you may be so engrossed in the organizational aspects that you forget to think outside of the box and miss out on the big picture.

The important thing to know is that neither style is better or smarter than the other. Each is simply different. The key to setting goals and reaching them is to understand where your shortcomings and strengths lie and when you have to adjust or push yourself to get the job done.

As the expression goes, "If you don't take care of the little things, the little things will take care of you." In other words, no dollar spent is insignificant, and mistakes such as letting loan payments slip can have exponential consequences. Building wealth means paying attention to the details, analyzing carefully and methodically. At the same time, you cannot reach your goals without thinking flexibly and creatively; there is almost always a solution that you haven't yet thought of and always more than one way of accomplishing the same goal. Keeping the big picture in sight is crucial.

A good thing for you to remember on your wealth-building journey is to act small and think big. In other words, believe in the ability of small, consistent steps to lead you to a major goal. This is a step-by-step, day-by-day process, but the purpose for your success encompasses ideals much larger than yourself. When Lewis was a college student, he kept an hour-by-hour schedule for his study, work, and free time, in order to fit it all in. At the bottom he wrote, "To be a good lawyer, one must study *hard*." His professional goal was always in sight, and the success that lay ahead of him would someday surpass even his expectations, benefiting generations of African Americans to come.

So, to answer our opening question, are some people born with more motivation than others? No. If you can understand why you're not getting started, you can begin to change your patterns of behavior. A dream to look forward to, a strong will, and careful self-reflection will all help to get you going and keep you on the track to financial empowerment.

Week 1: Exploring Your Goals

Assignment

Start a **spending record,** which you will keep for the entire month. Write down exactly what you spend every day. (This includes things as incidental as bottled water or a small cash loan to a friend.) Using a small spiral notebook, like a reporter's, is a good idea because you can take it with you wherever you go. Be faithful—this may seem tedious, but it is the only way to truly see where your money goes. Re-recording your entries into an Excel spreadsheet (or another computer software program) every few days will make it easier for you to tally your results in the end.

Take a guess at the start of any given day or week as to how much you will spend, and see how close you come. Note whether you went over or under your spending expectations.

_____

_____

_____

_____

_____

_____

_____

_____

_____

_____

_____

_____

_____

_____

_____

_____

What are the things, places, and people that inspire you? Give some thought to what your long-term dream is: Do you want to travel? Write a novel? Buy a home in the mountains? Learn how to fly a plane? What will motivate you?

The ultimate benefit of being successful is the luxury of giving yourself the time to do what you want to do.

—LEONTYNE PRICE
  PIONEERING CLASSICAL
  SOPRANO

_____

_____

_____

_____

_____

_____

_____

_____

_____

Tips for Procrastinators

People often assume procrastinators are lazy or indifferent to their responsibilities. But, in fact, some of the biggest procrastinators are also the biggest perfectionists. It is precisely because they want to do such a good job that they can't seem to get started. If there have been times you've been guilty of procrastination, read the following tips. If you don't need this advice, you're luckier than most of us. Share it with a friend who does.

1. **Tackle things day by day.** If you have something hanging over you, don't let a day go by without doing something toward accomplishing it, even if it is just making a phone call or creating a timeline.

2. **Conquer the task you like the least first.** Once you've gotten past what you dread, the rest will come easily.

3. **Plan a reward for yourself ahead of time.** For example: "If I spend two hours on my taxes today, I'll go see that new movie tonight."

4. **Procrastination is part of the process.** Be self-aware: If you are going to scrub the tub or watch an hour of television before you start your work, factor that time into your schedule.

5. **Know the difference between procrastination and productive thinking time.** Just because you're not typing away, that doesn't mean your mind is not doing important work. Allow yourself to think—but as soon as those insignificant daydreams take over, get up. Make some coffee. Take a brisk walk. Do whatever it takes to get your mind back on task.

6. **Set deadlines.** If you already have one, set a new one a week ahead. If you don't have a strict deadline, create one—and tell a friend or a coworker. Make a bet with a procrastinating friend on who will or won't make their deadline.

7. **Set yourself up to work.** A woman who kept putting off her daily jog after work began changing into her running clothes at five o'clock. It may sound like too simple a solution, but she felt pretty stupid drinking margaritas with her coworkers in a

jogging suit. So if you have paperwork to do, spread it out over the kitchen table first thing in the day or find a way to make your task an obstacle for your many distractions.

FIND YOURSELF MISSING BILL DEADLINES?

Check out www.paymybills.com, www.checkfree.com, or www.paytrust.com. These are a few of many new online service sites that will send you an e-mail when a bill is coming due, get your permission to make a payment, and click—it's done! (These companies charge monthly fees ranging from $4 to $15. Not for everyone, but less than some of those late fees.)

Week 2: Making It Real

Assignment

Get Real

Now that you've given some thought to your dream and your own very personal motive for financial empowerment, do some research. How much does that house cost, that degree, those lessons? If you want to write a novel, read a biography about your favorite novelist. In other words, make your dream seem real, while also finding out what it will take, realistically, to accomplish it.

When you think about your financial situation, what worries you? What are your worst fears?

_____

_____

_____

_____

_____

_____

_____

_____

_____

_____

_____

_____

_____

_____

_____

_____

> Impossibilities are merely things of which we have not learned, or which we do not wish to happen.
> —CHARLES W. CHESNUTT
>   WRITER

You've written it down. Now let it go.

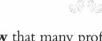

Did you know that many professional and Olympic athletes practice visualization, a technique that involves imagining yourself accomplishing your goal in your mind? One Olympic swimmer described bringing a stopwatch to bed at night, so that she could time her visualization of winning the gold medal in the 100-meter breaststroke. Eyes closed, stopwatch in hand, she visualized every detail of the race, the sound of the announcer's voice, the tiles on the bottom of the pool, the taste of the water, the touch of the wall, and her winning time on the scoreboard. It worked! She won the gold and set a world record.

Can you see yourself accomplishing your goal? Try to follow the swimmer's model and write down the details here.

_____

_____

_____

_____

_____

_____

_____

_____

_____

_____

_____

_____

_____

_____

_____

_____

_____

_____

_____

_____

_____

_____

See this image in your mind again and again. Whenever your focus blurs, call it clearly into view again.

Get Organized

There are now web sites that will help you get organized for free. Sometimes called "virtual secretaries," these sites provide such tools as calendars, notepads, and address books, all of which you can access through the World Wide Web anywhere in the world. The site www.bungo.com has the added option to share documents, public address books, event calendars, and bookmarks with other Bungo users. Other good organizers to check out are www.anyday .com, www.myevents.com, and www.officeclick.com.

I don't think of myself as a poor deprived ghetto girl who made good. I think of myself as someone who from an early age knew I was responsible for myself, and I had to make good.
—OPRAH WINFREY
MULTIMEDIA MAGNATE

Assignment

Complete the following quiz, and see where you stand.

Your Cognitive Style

Not sure which end of the continuum you are on? Try this quiz—it can give you a sense of which way your brain leans.

For each question, pick one answer (a, b, c, or d) which best describes you.

1. **When you are meeting a friend, you are**
   a. usually on time
   b. always on time, often early
   c. often 5 to 10 minutes late
   d. always 10 or more minutes late, no matter how hard you try not to be

2. **You find a crossword puzzle in the newspaper. You**
   a. enjoy them and are really good at them
   b. like them now and then
   c. can see the fun in them but don't always find yourself doing them
   d. find them irritating, can't understand why others like them

3. **When it comes to remembering historical dates, you are**
   a. uncannily good at it
   b. pretty good
   c. not very good
   d. really bad

4. **When it comes to the creative arts such as music, visual arts, and creative writing, you**
   a. have a talent
   b. really enjoy them but aren't good at them yourself
   c. aren't very interested in them
   d. find them somewhat pointless

5. **If someone asks you for directions you tend to**
   a. recite each step the person will have to make, including street names and estimates on distance traveled by blocks or mileage
   b. offer directions, not in so much detail, but with confidence that they are clear and correct
   c. find yourself hesitating and correcting yourself, worrying that the directions aren't altogether clear
   d. pretend you don't know the answer, even if you might—you're terrible at giving directions

6. **When receiving a bill in a restaurant, you**
   a. first check each item on the bill for errors and then take the time to calculate exactly the percentage that you want to leave
   b. look over the bill for glaring mistakes, then calculate the tip
   c. double the tax or use another quick technique to figure the tip
   d. look only at the total, leave what your gut tells you for a tip, sometimes going a bit over or under because you don't want to wait for change

7. **When traveling in a new city, you**
   a. always consult a map, determining each move ahead of time
   b. enjoy using maps efficiently and casually—after all, you have a good sense of direction
   c. are often confused by maps
   d. don't use maps and often find yourself lost, but make great discoveries along the way

8. **On Monday morning, a colleague asks about the movie you saw Saturday night. You**
   a. can easily recount the events of the movie from start to finish (if they want to hear it)
   b. offer the context (i.e., historical, political) and "what happens" before you get to characters
   c. talk about the relationships or themes before you talk about the plot

d. can't remember details (minor characters' names, plot twists); you're likely to describe how the movie made you feel

9. **It's tax time. Your attitude toward filling out tax forms is that**
   a. you're so good at it that you find yourself doing your friends' and family's taxes
   b. filing comes easily to you and it gives you a satisfying sense of accomplishment
   c. you really don't like it, get confused, and sometimes resort to getting outside help
   d. they make you crazy—you've missed the deadline more than once

10. **If you need to assemble a toy with directions, you**
    a. read through the written directions first, then follow them; the pictures aren't much help
    b. use both the written directions and the pictures, in the order they appear
    c. use only the pictures, sometimes skipping ahead
    d. try assembling the toy without directions

Those who most frequently answered "a" are on the left end of the continuum: analytic, careful, and logical. Those with mostly "d" answers are on the right end of the continuum: impulsive, rapid, and intuitive. Those with more "b" answers lean left; those with more "c" answers lean right.

Do you see yourself leaning one way or the other? Some people find themselves in the middle.

_____

_____

_____

_____

_____

Assignment

Flip ahead through the book, glancing over the questions, assignments for the week, and worksheets. Which look fun or interesting to you? Which seem unappealing, boring, or even aggravating? This should give you a sense of what comes naturally to you and what doesn't. Although this may seem obvious, making yourself aware now may stop you from putting down the journal at some time in the future, at the risk of relegating it to the back burner or quitting altogether. Instead you can say, "Oh, yes, here is another of those worksheets. I don't want to do it, but I will!"

Like: _____

_____

_____

_____

_____

Dread: _____

_____

_____

_____

_____

Can deal with: _____

_____

_____

_____

_____

_____

Now, mentally recommit to doing it all, because you can and because you will be so much better for it.

Sounds Risky . . .

If someone's behavior in the workplace was described as risky, would you think of that as a good thing or bad? Researchers who have made it their business to determine what corporations are looking for in making important hires today contend that risk taking is a highly desirable trait. Entrepreneurs, by definition, are comfortable with risk. Even in large corporations employees with entrepreneurial traits are favored, because they show a bias toward action and make conscious decisions not to be stopped by typical bureaucratic and political obstacles. Rules and red tape are out. Innovation and political accountability are in.

Are you a risk taker? A thrill seeker? Or are you afraid of taking risks? Think about a recent time when you went out on a limb and it paid off. Now think about a mistake you've made. How did you react emotionally? How did you handle it publicly? How much does what other people think about you factor into your decision to try something you're not sure will work?

> I really don't think life is about the I-could-have-beens. Life is only about the I-tried-to-do. I don't mind the failure but I can't imagine that I'd forgive myself if I didn't try.
> —NIKKI GIOVANNI
>   WRITER AND POET

Assignment

Prepare to Begin

Get yourself in the right mind-set, and start thinking financially. Whether personal finance is a new subject to you or you already know quite a bit about it, there's always a lot to learn. Read publications such as *Black Enterprise,* the *Wall Street Journal,* and weekly business magazines. Browse the bookstore for personal finance guides that meet your needs. Prick up your ears when there is talk of personal finance at the office or among friends and family— don't retreat from it, even if it seems over your head. Ask successful people how they did it and what lessons they learned from their mistakes. This week—and always—keep a record of the new things you've learned, as well as concepts that you don't yet understand. Start a clippings file for articles you find pertinent.

What are at least three things you've learned about finance this week? What concepts do you still need to learn more about?

_____

_____

_____

_____

> Life is a grindstone, but whether it grinds you down or polishes you up depends on what you are made of.
> —ROBERT E. JOHNSON
> ENTREPRENEUR

Add It Up

Tally your expenditures. Itemize them. Try to be as detailed as possible when categorizing. For example, find out how much you spend per week or per month on afternoon snacks or ordering out lunch at the office. How much do you spend on clothes? You will see a picture of your spending patterns begin to form as you look over your totals.

Lead, don't follow. Don't be afraid to go it alone. Don't be afraid to lose. Don't be afraid to ask questions. Don't be afraid.
—WILLIAM M. LEWIS JR.
INVESTMENT BANKING
EXECUTIVE

_____
_____
_____
_____
_____
_____
_____
_____
_____

By now you have a sense of your spending—reflect on it. What surprised you most? When do you splurge? When do you spend more than you should, whether impulsively or simply to save time? Where can you cut back?

_____
_____
_____
_____
_____
_____

Challenge/Goal

Become a *conscious* spender.

The Web is a great source for up-to-date information on business. Check out www.cbs.marketwatch.com, www.forbes.com, www.blackenterprise.com, www.djinterative.com. (Dow Jones Interactive), www.ft.com (*Financial Times*), www.business-wire.com, and countless others. **Organize your bookmarks.** Check out www.blink.com, a free bookmarking site that allows you to access your bookmarks from any computer.

Notes

> The great challenge is to prepare ourselves to enter these doors of opportunity.
> —REV. MARTIN LUTHER KING JR.
> NOBEL PEACE PRIZE WINNER AND CIVIL RIGHTS LEADER

from Black Enterprise, *February 2000*

Mirian M. Graddick, executive vice president of human resources, was the only woman on AT&T's senior leadership team, the body responsible for the telecommunication giant's strategy and direction. Named executive vice president of human resources in March 1999, Graddick, 46, was responsible for the design, planning, and administration of programs for more than 150,000 employees in the United States and around the world.

Graddick began her affiliation with AT&T after graduating from Hampton University. She worked as an intern for two consecutive summers in Bell Laboratories' research group, which motivated the aspiring clinical psychologist to pursue a business career. After winning a Bell Labs scholarship for women and minorities, she pursued an advanced degree, eventually completing her doctoral studies at Penn State in industrial/organizational psychology. Graddick joined AT&T in the early 1980s and moved up through the ranks, holding a variety of management positions in human resources.

Graddick credits much of her success to being able to quickly embrace change. She says, "You must be willing to learn new things and have the ability to get out of your comfort zone and enhance yourself professionally."

Graddick advises younger colleagues to learn from their mistakes and move on to the next project. "I tell the people I coach that at the end of the day, you're judged not by what happens in a particular situation, but how you react to that situation and how you apply what you learn."

Saving Your Money

William M. Lewis Jr. was the first African American to achieve the position of managing director at the high-powered Wall Street firm Morgan Stanley Dean Witter and Company. He holds a BA and an MBA from Harvard University. Even as a child, Lewis possessed the traits that would carry him through his many successes in life.

"My first real job was raking leaves at the convent in front of the house I grew up in," he says. "Everybody would be out playing, and I would be there, brushing leaves. . . . I always liked that routine and the knowledge that I was going to get paid every Saturday morning. I was always a saver, and, to me, that was just money in the bank. Even back then, I knew that I wanted a future very different from what I saw in inner-city Richmond, Virginia. I was already hungry at age seven."

As a high school student, Lewis took part in the A Better Chance program, an organization that he has remained devoted to. He attended Andover Academy, where he felt the most obvious difference between him and the other kids was material, but he didn't allow that discrepancy to get him down. "I just didn't dwell on what I didn't have," he explains. "I focused on what I had. I mean, as a child I wanted more than to be poor in Richmond, but it wasn't because I wasn't happy, or because I felt lesser than anybody else. I simply knew there was a lot more to be had and so I was a striver."

Striving means saving. Getting in the habit of effectively saving your money is the most essential lesson you can learn on this journey. As Lewis eloquently put it, wanting to get ahead financially doesn't have to be about being unhappy in your life or being driven by envy. Saving your money is a way of showing respect for what you do and for who you are, and it's about believing that you have the capacity within yourself to one day have more for you, your family, and your community.

The basic rule of thumb is that you should be saving 10 to 15 percent of your after-tax income. This is in addition to your 401(k), IRA, or other retirement savings plan. Signing the Declaration of Financial Empowerment means making this vow, first and foremost. This chapter is designed to teach even those of you who are living paycheck to paycheck concrete ways to change your life so that you can make saving money a habit, as second nature to you as brushing your teeth. The most important thing is to begin, right away, even if you need to start out with less than 10 percent.

What are the reasons for making saving a priority? First, we all need to save for retirement. Most people these days live 20 years into their retirements, and we can't depend on Social Security alone. According to the American Savings Retirement Council, benefits will play a more limited role in the retirement picture, as the age to receive maximum benefits will rise to 66 in 2005 and to 67 in 2022. Today, Social Security pays only 27 percent of final pay to a worker who earned $60,000 a year, 42 percent to someone who earned $40,000, and 56 percent of a $20,000 salary. Some analysts believe that benefits will need to be reduced and retirement age raised even further, before many of today's workers reach retirement. So if you want to have that comfortable retirement you've always imagined or, in some cases, if you simply don't want to experience financial hardships after you stop working, you need to make retirement savings a priority.

When do you plan to retire? What kind of a life do you expect to have? What are the specific things you've always hoped to be able to do after you retire?

In the first chapter we explored having a financial goal. Saving for that house or boat you've always dreamed of or just getting yourself out of debt are fulfilling and worthwhile pursuits. But what's even more important—and what most people overlook—is that you need to save money simply to protect yourself from the unexpected. Everyone needs to have an emergency fund for such unfortunate expenses as medical bills, loss of job, death in the family, or legal fees. No one wants to think about these kinds of things, but if you are at least prepared financially, you'll be in a better position to help yourself and your family through a hard time. Ideally, your fund should cover six months' living expenses, kept in a savings account or money market account that you can access at any time.

Saving requires time and consistency. Simply put, to save more money you need to decrease your spending and/or increase your earnings. In this chapter you'll focus on budgeting your money to make those spending cuts possible, and you'll look at ways to reduce your existing expenses.

The first step in controlling your spending is to pay yourself first. If you can, have your employer deduct a set amount from each paycheck and have it deposited directly into your savings. If the money's not there, you can't spend it. It's as simple as that. If you can't arrange for such a system, get in the habit of writing a check to your savings account at each paycheck, even before you pay any bills.

In the days ahead, you'll also be asked to examine your spending habits, from big expenditures to small indulgences. More than anything, you should try to become mindful of your spending. If you want to splurge on something, go ahead. But just make sure you can afford it, you've chosen carefully, and you're getting the best price out there. You should also give some thought to what you pay other people to do for you that you could do for yourself. We live in a service-driven culture where virtually everything from running your errands to mowing your lawn to painting your toenails can be done by someone else, for a price. You should think about which services you can do without.

At the beginning of this month, you will create a formal budget for yourself. Use the observations you made about your spending in Chapter 1 to plan ahead. For example, if you've discovered that you spend too much money at that take-out restaurant you love so much, put a cap on it. You can still get your favorite items, but you'll have to cut back on impulse purchases.

The last task of this chapter will be to begin to think about how you can increase your income. Are you making the most money you can at work? We will take a closer look at your earning potential in Chapter 8, but now is the time to start asking yourself whether you could be making more money in your current position or getting supplementary income by taking on an outside job or project.

Finally, once you're saving money, you need to make sure you're getting the best return on it. This requires research to determine which method is best for you. Keep reading those financial publications and web sites, and don't forget to ask around for advice. Most important, never lose sight of the big picture. If saving your money doesn't seem as exciting as spending it, think about the excitement of true financial empowerment and the sense of accomplishment that comes with striving for a better future each day. Also, keep visualizing that long-term goal. It's the sound short-term choices you make each day that will get you there—or push your goal farther away. Reach for it!

Week 1: Reducing Spending

Getting Educated about Saving

Uncle Sam is one of your best resources. The Savings Are Vital to Everyone Act of 1997 (SAVER) laid out a congressional mandate for the Department of Labor to make the education of Americans about retirement savings a priority. As a result, there are very accessible, very informative resources available at www.dol.gov/dol/pwba or (800) 998-7542 for the Department of Labor and www.CFP-Board.org or (888) 237-6275 for the Certified Financial Planner Board of Standards.

Take another look at your spending record. Divide expenditures into two categories: *necessary* and *unnecessary.* Think about your spending beyond the essentials. Why do you buy these things? What could you do without? What *should* you do without? Now try to figure out why you spend this money. Does shopping make you feel happy when you're down? Do those items make you feel more important, attractive, cool? Think about what you could do that's free, such as going for a walk or jog, that could bring out the same—or better—results. Create a list of alternatives to replace the habits that detract from your goal—for example, "Every time I'm tempted to impulse shop, I'll call a friend or read a book."

_____

_____

_____

_____

_____

_____

_____

_____

_____

_____

_____

_____

_____

_____

Manhattan was a real scorcher during July and August of 1968. I found an apartment, a five-floor walkup on 21 Street on the west side of Manhattan. It had one bedroom and the rent was $150 a month. I could afford a lot more . . . but the idea of saving as much as possible was irresistible.
—REGINALD F. LEWIS
    *WHY SHOULD WHITE GUYS
    HAVE ALL THE FUN?*

How expensive is your fun? You don't need to go out to a five-star restaurant to have a romantic night. Make finding the best-kept secrets a challenge. List ways you and your friends or family can have a good time without spending a lot of money.

_____

_____

_____

_____

_____

_____

_____

_____

_____

> We quickly learned the meaning of sound money management. We didn't track our cash flow properly, and moved into a big, impressive office. Within months, we were unable to pay rent and we were kicked out. From that point on, we kept our options small and tight.
> —RUSSELL SIMMONS
> ENTREPRENEUR

When you pay for services, which are lifesavers, which are mere conveniences, and which are beyond unnecessary? What could you start doing yourself (i.e., cooking instead of going out, changing your oil, or doing your nails) that you now pay someone else to do?

_____

_____

_____

_____

_____

_____

_____

_____

_____

Shopping in Bulk

Do you just love a bargain? If so, you probably frequent one of those price club stores where everything from electronics to soap and frozen foods comes in big sizes at reduced prices. But this kind of shopping can be a double-edged sword. We've all come home with something we don't need, just because the price was good. Be realistic and reflective. Buy only what you *need*. It helps to know before you walk into those towers of gleaming new products exactly what you plan to buy, so make a list and stick to it! If you're smart about it, you can save up to 40 percent on basic items and have storage space to spare.

Assignment

Design Your Own Monthly Budget

You can use a software budgeting program such as Quicken or Microsoft Money, an Excel spreadsheet, or just an accountant's notebook and a calculator. **Whichever suits you, be specific and detailed.** First, determine your monthly income, including factors such as average tips or bonuses, alimony payments, or investment income. Then, determine your spending, allowing for your savings deductions. Having closely examined where your money goes (Chapter 1), you should be able to account for everything in your budget. At the beginning of each month you will draw up a new budget. It may take a few months to work out the kinks, but soon you will have true control over where your money goes. Keep in mind that carefully plotting a budget takes time. Set a little time aside each week to review your spending. This will help a lot when you sit down at the beginning of the next month to create a new budget.

TIP Not only do most banks charge you fees for each ATM transaction beyond a minimum number each month, but other banks and ATM providers will charge fees as high as $1.75 per transaction on top of your bank's fee. Monitor and minimize your

ATM withdrawals. Decide ahead of time how much cash you will need for the week and make one withdrawal. This can help with sporadic spending and keep you on your budget. Go a step further and keep a running tab of your ATM fees for one month. What else might you have done with that money?

_____

_____

_____

_____

_____

_____

_____

_____

_____

_____

_____

_____

_____

_____

_____

_____

_____

_____

Financial Calculators

Let web sites do the math for you. Check out www.money.com, moneycentral.msn.com, and www.financenter.com, among many others.

Worksheet

How much do you actually need to set aside each year to achieve retirement goals?

Retirement Planning

1. Your current annual income   _____

2. Your desired annual income after retirement   _____

3. Estimated Social Security and pension income   _____

4. Income you'll need from personal savings (#2 − #3) = _____

5. At what age would you like to retire?   _____

6. Determine your income multiple from the following table: _____

Retirement age	50–54	55–59	60–64	65+
Income multiple	26	23	20	17

7. Necessary personal savings (#5 × #6) =   _____

This is your *retirement savings goal.*

HOW TO REACH YOUR GOAL

8. What is your total personal savings now?   _____

9. Determine your growth multiple from the following table: _____

Years until retirement	8	12	16	20	24
Growth multiple	2	3	4	5	6

10. Estimated value of current personal savings at retirement (#8 × #9) =   _____

11. Current savings shortfall (#7 − #10) =   _____

12. Determine savings factor from the following table: _____

Approximate years to retirement	8	12	16	20	24
Savings factor	0.100	0.070	0.045	0.032	0.025

13. Annual savings necessary (#12 × #11) =   _____

The ABCs of Retirement Savings

Here are some of your best options.

Defined-Contribution Plans

Many companies are replacing the older typical pension plan (defined-benefit plans) in which the employer pays a lump sum or a guaranteed monthly payment after retirement with defined-contribution plans. In these plans the employees can contribute savings to a fund each month, which the company then invests. Unlike the defined-benefit plans, these don't guarantee a specific amount after retirement—that amount will depend on how much you have put away each month, for how long, and how the investments faired. Though the federal government doesn't guarantee the specific amount you will accumulate, it does protect your money from misuse by the employer. The most important distinction is that in most cases employers match employee contributions. This is free money!

401(k) Plans

This is the most common of the contribution plans, and it allows you to invest your money automatically. Most employers will match 25 cents for each dollar you put in. You also receive significant tax breaks. First of all, your savings and earnings are deferred from income tax until you take out the money. This helps your nest egg grow faster. Second, the money is taken out of your paycheck before taxes. Everything you put away is tax-free income. (The maximum contribution allowed each year is usually around 15 percent of your salary.)

403(b) Plans

These are 401(k) plans for those who work for nonprofit or public organizations. Investments are made in tax-free annuities or mutual funds.

Profit-Sharing Plans and Employee Stock Ownership Plans (ESOP)

In these plans employers share company assets with their employees, either through profits or company stock.

Start Your Own Plan

If contribution plans aren't available to you, you can start your own plan.

Individual Retirement Accounts (IRAs)

You can make deductible IRA contributions of up to $2,000 annually if your income is under $100,000. (You can put aside an additional $2,000 per year for a nonworking spouse if you file your taxes together.) Many banks, mutual fund companies, insurance companies, and other financial service providers offer IRA accounts. In some cases, you may be eligible to deduct all or part of your IRA contributions from your income before taxes.

SIMPLE-IRA

This is the Savings Incentive Match Plan for Employees of Small Employers.

Annuities

This is an arrangement you make with an insurance company, a brokerage firm, a bank, or another financial services organization, in which you pay them installments in return for either a fixed amount when you retire or a sum that reflects how much your investments earned. This is called a **variable annuity.** Earnings aren't taxed until you withdraw them. Unlike the IRA accounts, there is no limit to how much money you can set aside, but these accounts come with other tax complications you should investigate.

Assignment

Make an appointment with your human resources representative to investigate exactly which retirement savings plans are available to you and when. If you are self-employed or don't have incentive plans available to you, make an appointment with a financial organization to look into the options listed here.

Caveat

If you are tempted by the attractive rates offered for you to borrow from your retirement account, beware. Borrowing will reduce the account earnings, and if you fail to pay back the loan, you could be subject to paying income tax and penalties.

Know Your Rights

The Social Security Administration now provides individualized Social Security statements that document the earnings on which you have paid Social Security taxes during your working years, along with a summary of the estimated benefits you'll receive. If you are 25 or older and aren't already receiving social security benefits, the statement is supposed to be mailed to you about three months before your birthday. To get your statement at any time, contact the Social Security Administration at (800) 772-1213 or request it online at www.ssa.gov.

Youth Is Wasted on the Young . . .

You have one huge ally—time. Let's say that you put $1,000 at the beginning of each year into an IRA from age 20 through age 30 (11 years) and then never put in another dime. The account earns 7 percent annually. When you retire at age 65 you'll have $168,514 in the account. A friend doesn't start until age 30, but saves the same amount annually for 35 years straight. Despite putting in three times as much money, your friend's account grows only to $147,913.

If you find yourself in the opposite situation, retirement is fast approaching and you haven't saved enough, here are some late-in-the-game suggestions for a retirement savings comeback:

- Sock it away. Pump everything you can into your tax-sheltered retirement plans and personal savings. Try to put away at least 20 percent of your income.

- Take a second job or work extra hours.

- Aim for higher returns. Don't invest in anything you are uncomfortable with, but see if you can squeeze out better returns.

- Retire later. You may not need to work full time beyond your planned retirement age. Part time may be enough.

- Delay the Social Security. Benefits will be higher when you start taking them.

- Make use of your home. Rent out a room or move to a less expensive home and save the profits.

- Sell assets that are not producing much income or growth, such as underdeveloped land or a vacation home, and invest in income-producing assets.

From *Saving Fitness: A Guide to Your Money and Financial Future,* published by the U.S. Department of Labor.

TIP Did you know that women live five to seven years longer than men on average? That means women need to save more for retirement.

Getting the Bad Stuff out on Paper

It sometimes helps to lay out all your negative feelings toward an endeavor. That way, you can see what may stop you from getting important business taken care of.

As you're investigating your retirement savings options, do things look bright or grim? What aspects of retirement savings are most worrisome to you?

_____

_____

_____

_____

_____

_____

_____

_____

_____

_____

_____

_____

_____

_____

_____

_____

_____

_____

_____

Anticipate the good so that you may enjoy it.
—ETHIOPIAN PROVERB

Rethink some financial sacrifices you may need to make, but also consider the payoff and sense of accomplishment you'll get from practicing sound financial judgment.

Week 3: Making the Most of Your Savings

Assignment

This week you are going to set up your auxiliary savings, the money you put aside in addition to your retirement savings. Do some research (on the Web, in financial publications, banking brochures) on where and how to put away your savings. Make appointments to meet with a few bank officers. Compare credit unions, passbook savings, certificates of deposit, insured money market accounts, money market mutual funds, and savings bonds. Then decide the best possible place for your money. Your decision will take into account how much you have to start, how accessible the savings need to be, and how the going interest rates on various savings vehicles compare. Keep track of what you've learned here.

_____

_____

_____

_____

_____

_____

_____

_____

_____

_____

_____

_____

_____

_____

_____

_____

> I don't focus on new beginnings only at the start of a new year. If I feel like I'm in a rut any time of the year, I get very focused on the idea that each new day offers the chance for a fresh start.
> —ROBIN ROBERTS
> SPORTSCASTER AND
> JOURNALIST

TIP When you open your emergency fund account, try to avoid monthly maintenance fees (sometimes tallying more than $100 per year) by inquiring about maintaining a minimum balance. Try to find a bank or credit union that employs an average daily balance method instead of a minimum daily balance. Another strategy for avoiding fees is to link the savings to a checking account.

Visit www.treasurydirect.com and www.savingsbonds.com for more information on government-sponsored savings.

Are You Adequately Insured?

Insurance is like a powerful cure for a deadly disease—nobody wants it until they need it. Then they want it desperately. Investing a little each month in the proper insurance can potentially save you from financial disaster down the road.

HEALTH INSURANCE

Compare the health plans available to you. Think about your own and your family's health care needs and decide which program is best for you. If your employer doesn't offer health insurance, you *must* look into getting at least catastrophic medical coverage on your own.

RENTER'S INSURANCE

Home owners are insured against fire, theft, and other liabilities. If you rent, you're not, but renter's insurance is very affordable. Look into it.

Also investigate and compare **disability insurance, life insurance,** and **umbrella insurance** policies.

TIP Installing insulation and weather stripping can cut heating and air-conditioning costs by as much as 50 percent.

Success Story

from Black Enterprise, *March 2000*

Lorenzo Richardson, a 29-year-old accountant, attributes his stellar savings record—he has very little student loan debt, adds an additional amount to his monthly mortgage payment, and is socking away money for an early retirement—to lessons learned from growing up on welfare. "We did what we had to do to make ends meet, like clip coupons, walk an extra mile or two to the store to get the best bargains," says Richardson, who is the oldest in a single-parent family of six.

At 17 he got his first part-time job at a consumer catalog show-room, where he made $3.75 an hour. With financial aid covering the majority of his college costs between 1988 and 1993 he accumulated $10,000 from part-time jobs, which he used as a down payment on a home in his native Jersey City. Of his current $38,000 salary, he contributes the maximum allowed—15 percent—to the company's 401(k) plan. He is also taking advantage of Panasonic's tuition reimbursement program to work toward an MBA.

To help turn his dream of retiring early and running his own business into a reality, about a year ago Richardson joined RDS Investment Club. He began by contributing $25 a month, but soon increased it to $100. As of November 1999, the club members enjoyed an annual compound return of 42 percent on their investments. On his own, Richardson is looking to buy shares in GE, Home Depot, and Wal-Mart via those companies' dividend reinvestment plans (DRIPs).

Next on Richardson's agenda is getting his mother and younger brothers and sister into the habit of saving and investing. In fact, the family has agreed to give each other shares of stock instead of other gifts for birthdays and Christmas.

Taking the Plunge!

Now that you are starting the process of setting up your savings, how do you feel? What are your concerns? What do you need to remind yourself of for the rest of the year—and beyond—in order to keep your hands out of the cookie jar?

_____

_____

_____

_____

_____

_____

_____

_____

_____

_____

_____

_____

_____

_____

_____

_____

_____

_____

_____

_____

_____

Assignment

> My father always stressed focusing on the things you can control. He said, "Your own performance you can control. No one can take that away from you."
> —KENNETH CHENAULT
> CORPORATE EXECUTIVE

First, investigate how your salary compares to the market rate. Do some research to find out how much other people in similar positions are making. Check the want ads and call employment agencies to inquire about salaries. If you're self-employed, find out what others charge for the same services you provide. Check out www.jobsmart.org or www.salarysource.com, among others. There you will find data on salaries for people with similar positions, credentials, and experience.

How does your salary stack up against the current market rate? Set a salary goal for yourself.

_____

_____

_____

_____

_____

_____

_____

Second, start preparing yourself for a raise. Are you the best employee you can be? Even little things like getting to work a few minutes early, asking to take on new projects, or showing a general enthusiasm around the office can go a long way toward improving the impression you make in the workplace. Start now, not three weeks before your annual review.

What can you do better at work?

_____

_____

_____

_____

_____

_____

_____

_____

Do you have a skill set (for example, child care or tutoring) that could bring in extra income? What resources do you have (i.e., property to rent or sell) that you're not taking advantage of?

Smooth seas do not make skillful sailors.
—AFRICAN PROVERB

_____

_____

_____

_____

_____

_____

_____

_____

_____

_____

_____

_____

_____

_____

TIP Are you taking advantage of everything your employer has to offer? Many benefits packages include tax-free accounts for such expenditures as public transit, parking, medical bills, and child care. These programs allow you to set aside tax-free dollars for monthly expenses. For example, an employer provides you with a transit account for expenses up to $65 per month. They deduct the amount you spend on transit from your paycheck before taxes, and then reimburse you each month. That comes to $780 of tax-free income per year.

Rethinking Your Lifestyle

Whether you are in a financial crunch or living comfortably, it could help to rethink big expenditures that have become an integral part of your life. How much do you spend each month on a mortgage or rent? It should be approximately one-quarter of your monthly income. If it's a lot more, you may want to consider moving to a more modest living space or to a less expensive location. What kind of car do you drive? Could you get by just as well in a more modest car without those high monthly payments? Do you have a high cell phone bill? _Is there excess in your life that you don't consider excess?_ Give it some thought.

Managing Debt and Credit

While still in his early twenties, John H. Johnson laid out a plan to begin publishing a magazine for African Americans. He eventually grew his business into a multi-million-dollar company. Here's how he got his start: "I was able to convince a loan company to loan me $500 on my mother's furniture, which we used as collateral. I used it to buy direct mail literature, which I sent out to 20,000 names from insurance companies. Three thousand answered and sent me $2.00 each, and with $6,000 I published my first edition of *Negro Digest* in 1942." Publisher and CEO of Johnson Publishing Company, Johnson counts the magazines *Ebony* and *Jet* among his many successes.

We chose the story of *Negro Digest* to begin this chapter to illustrate what we call "good debt" and as a very basic example of leveraging assets to move yourself forward. This month we address debt and credit. This is the last step before you roll up your sleeves and focus on investing. Before you can allocate money toward the stock market, you need to pay down your debt.

There's good debt and bad debt. A mortgage is an example of good debt for several reasons: You're not throwing away money on rent each month; you've made an investment in something that most likely will appreciate over time; you've opened yourself up to the credit benefits of being a home owner, and you're receiving the U.S. government's single biggest tax break for individuals—tax deductions on mortgage interest payments—to boot! Good debt is also a loan that improves your position or earning power.

In today's world, it's impossible to imagine life without any kind of debt or credit transaction. Most people can't pay outright for a home, a secondary education, or a new car. If you want to start your own business, chances are you will have to take out a loan. Traveling is almost impossible without the security of a credit card and everyday transactions such as opening an account at a video store, renting a car, or making a purchase online all require credit cards. Whether we like it or not, credit and debt play some role in everyone's financial life.

With that said, misusing credit and failing to look debt in the face are often the toughest obstacles to building wealth. If you're guilty of poor credit practices, you're not alone. Credit card debt is a widespread problem among Americans. If you find yourself paying only the minimum on your bills, maxing out credit cards, getting charged late fees, or borrowing from your card to pay regular bills or other loans, you've got bad credit habits. This month, you will take a close and hard look at the role debt plays in your financial life, and you will make a change for the better.

Have you ever borrowed money from a friend or family member that you couldn't pay back as soon as you would have liked? How did that make you feel? Are you carrying debt that's gnawing at you? How does it affect your mind-set and your financial confidence?

_____

_____

_____

_____

_____

_____

Don't despair. Thinking about debt is a sobering endeavor that could put almost anyone in a bad mood. But over time, even the worst credit ratings can be repaired. If your debt is substantial, you should employ the saving techniques described in Chapter 2, but contribute the money directly to paying off your debt. It makes sense. Look at it this way: Paying off a credit card with 18 percent interest is like getting $18 tax free for every $100 you pay off. That's a better return than you get from the average stock market, and that's precisely why you shouldn't be investing funds when you have significant debt to pay off. It's counterproductive.

Good advice for anyone, regardless of your debt situation, is to avoid using your credit card whenever possible. Almost all banks now offer debit cards. You get the same convenience, but the money comes directly out of your checking account. When using credit, limit yourself to one or two cards, paying off the cards that hold the highest interest rates first.

If you can, pay off your expenditures on your credit card each month, or at least the most sizable amount you can afford. (If you pay only the minimum 2 percent on a $2,000 balance with 18 percent interest, it will take you 15 years to pay it off!) Finally, pay *all* of your bills on time. A history of late payments shows up on your credit report and will ultimately prevent you from making significant financial strides.

To be financially viable you must establish a good credit rating. Think about all the instances in which your credit history will be checked: if you want to buy a home, secure a business loan, establish a utility account, apply to rent an apartment, buy a car, even start a new job. One of the goals of this journey is to keep bad credit from getting in the way of your living your life the way you want to. Having good credit means you have buying power, and the security of that translates into personal power. If you store your credit, you will be free to use it in case of an emergency or to take advantage of the right time to buy something.

Those of you who are starting out or starting over can absolutely build a good credit rating for yourself. It takes diligence and time. For those of you who are in good shape debt-wise, keep it up—you've won half the battle. If you're smart about it, and the opportunity arises, you'll be prepared to leverage your assets in a responsible, successful way.

Assignment

> Once in debt, it's no easy matter for a whole race to emerge.
> —W.E.B. DuBois
> Scholar and founding member, NAACP

Everyone should know what his or her credit rating is. It's a good idea to view your credit report once a year. Request your credit rating from one of the three major credit-reporting agencies. You may have to pay a fee of around $8, but some states have laws requiring agencies to provide you with one free report every year. Because these three are competing companies, they may not have identical information about you. If you want to be thorough, order a report from each company.

Equifax: (800) 685-1111, www.equifax.com

Experian: (888) 397-3742, www.experian.com

Trans Union Corporation: (800) 916-8800, www.transunion.com

More Than Those Student Loans to Worry About

Did you know that the fastest-growing population of consumers racking up credit card debt is college students? Credit card companies are targeting undergraduates with aggressive campaigns. Many students find themselves with several different accounts, paying for books and other necessities with their new-found credit, only to have amassed thousands of dollars of debt by graduation.

Think about how you use your credit card. How does it feel different from pulling out cash or writing a check and balancing your checkbook? Look through your credit card bills. Are you reflective enough about the purchases you make on your card? How can you do better?

_____

_____

_____

_____

_____

_____

_____

_____

_____

_____

_____

Know Your Rights

Under the Fair Credit Reporting Act, you have the right to:

- Receive a copy of your credit report, containing all of the information in your file at the time of your request.

- Know the name of anyone who received your credit report in the last year for most purposes or in the last two years for employment purposes.

- Obtain a free copy of your credit report when your application is denied because of information supplied by a credit reporting agency, if your request is made within 60 days of receiving your denial notice.

- Contest the completeness or accuracy of information in your report.

- Add a summary explanation to your credit report if your dispute is not resolved to your satisfaction.

> If we are to survive today and realize the dream of our mission, we must somehow keep the means by which we live abreast with the ends for which we live.
> —REV. MARTIN LUTHER KING JR.

Assignment

Complete the following worksheet.

Debt Ratio Worksheet

How much are your monthly loan bills?*

1. Car loans   _____

2. Student loans   _____

3. Minimum credit card payments combined   _____

4. Charge card loan   _____

5. Personal loans   _____

6. Any other loans, including seller financing (such as a boat loan) and asset-based loans   _____

7. Total of #1–#6   _____

What is your annual income?

8. Annual salary, after taxes   _____

9. Bonuses   _____

10. Self-employment income

11. Net income from rental properties   _____

12. Interest

13. Dividends   _____

14. Any other miscellaneous income, such as parental support or educational scholarships   _____

15. Total of #8–#14   _____

16. Divide #15 by #12   _____

17. Divide #7 by #16. Your debt ratio =   _____

Your answer should be equal to 10 percent or less.

*Do you have outstanding debt (student loans or unpaid bills) that you are not paying each month? If so, estimate them and include them in your calculations for item #6.

How did you fare with your debt ratio? What is your personal reaction? If your ratio is above 10 percent, why do you think that is? Brainstorm ways to reduce it. If your ratio is below 10, brainstorm ways to keep yourself there.

_____

_____

_____

_____

_____

_____

_____

_____

_____

_____

_____

_____

Feeling Overwhelmed by Your Debt?

There are nonprofit organizations that provide credit counseling. Check out www.creditcounseling.org, www.myvesta.org, or www .needhelpwithbills.org. But **be warned:** There are many for-profit "credit repair" companies that offer to erase bad credit history for a fee. This can't be done. *Only you* can repair your own credit by paying off your debts.

TIP **Make That Call.** If you are going to be late with a bill payment of any kind, call the vendor *before* the bill is past due. Creditors, especially student loan companies, don't want you to go into default. Offering a reasonable explanation and setting up an alternative payment plan will keep that lapse off your credit report.

> It is difficult for me to think of any situation that is more trying on the nerves than [that] of [having] heavy financial obligations to meet, without knowing where the money is to come from to meet those obligations month to month.
> —BOOKER T. WASHINGTON
> EDUCATOR AND ORATOR

Have you received your credit report yet? If not, follow up on your inquiry.

❧

If you don't own a home and are interested in looking into buying one, visit www.fanniemae.com. The Fannie Mae foundation offers three free brochures: a credit guide, a borrowing guide, and a home-buying guide.

TIP Consider paying for your next car in cash. You will avoid paying 11 percent or so in interest. Remember that new cars aren't good investments. A good chunk of the car's value disappears the moment you drive it off the lot. This will, of course, mean choosing a less expensive new car or a used car you can afford. It will make your car insurance much cheaper as well.

> My business is successful, but real success to me means having balance and peace of mind, and I'm still working on that. That's the meaningful part of the equation for me.
> —TERRIE WILLIAMS
> ENTREPRENEUR

Success Story

from Black Enterprise, *October 1999*

M. Starita Boyce, Ed.D., has always believed that achieving one's financial goals takes hard work, solid investments, and time. Boyce, a 40-year-old who develops community programs and inner-city initiatives for the American Bible Society, has been saving as far back as she can remember. She recalls receiving an allowance from her father and savings bonds, as Christmas presents, from her grandfather. Her mother then took her to open a Christmas fund at a local bank when she was barely tall enough to reach the teller's window. By the age of 12, she was saving money through her account at Carver Savings in Brooklyn—and proud of banking with a black-owned financial institution. (Now renamed Carver Bancorp Inc., the institution is No. 1 on the BE banks list and is on the BE Black Stock Index.)

By 1981, Boyce had opened an individual retirement account, but she cashed it out around 1988 to pay for her doctoral studies. By the time she received her doctorate in education with a concentration in finance in 1992, Boyce was in debt to the tune of $40,000 in student loans and about $7,000 in credit card bills.

After reviewing her statements and calculating how much she would end up paying back if she stuck to the minimum payment schedules, she came to realize she would pay two or three times what she'd borrowed. Instead, Boyce devised a plan: She sent in a check every other week and attached a note specifying that the payment was to be applied to her principal balance outstanding. This way, Boyce saved tens of thousands of dollars in finance charges, and she knocked off all of her debt in less than 10 years.

Along the way, Boyce says, she restricted unnecessary spending. "When my girlfriends were going to Bermuda and getting manicures, I didn't," she says. "I learned to sacrifice and appreciate the free things in New York."

Boyce now has $30,000 saved for retirement. She invests nearly $5,000 annually in a 403(b) plan—the nonprofit equivalent of a 401(k)—and her employer matches those contributions. She also puts her annual tax refund into a Roth IRA. And, because she is single, she has put aside an emergency fund that would pay her mortgage for 10 months in the event she is disabled or suddenly loses her job.

Although none of us can predict what our health will be like in our later years, Boyce has a clear vision of her future as a retiree. "My retirement gift to myself, hopefully, will be a boat," Boyce says. She would like to sail to different ports around the country and enjoy serene evenings cruising the waters and eating fine cuisine. "I find water to be very calming and I would like to have as stress-free a life as possible. That's what I look forward to in retirement— just enjoying life."

Take a Deep Breath

Give yourself a break from the numbers and remind yourself of your dreams. Think about and describe how financial empowerment will change your life and the lives of the people you care for.

_____

_____

_____

_____

_____

_____

_____

_____

_____

_____

_____

_____

_____

_____

_____

Assignment

Take Out Your Scissors

Eliminate all but two of your credit cards. If you need to, lay out a plan for yourself to pay off the cards with the highest interest rates first, then close those accounts. If you've never used credit, your assignment is different. Begin to put together what's called a "nontraditional credit history." Keep copies of all the bills you pay (including rent) and copies of the canceled checks. Ask your landlord and utilities companies to write a letter vouching for your record of paying bills on time. Finally, look into getting a credit card. It may seem contradictory, but using a card responsibly can help to build a credit record for you. If you're really credit shy, opt for a debit card at least.

Week 4: Analyzing Your Credit Report

Assignment

By now, you should have your credit report in hand. Take the time to read it over carefully, and make sure you understand it. If you have *any* questions, jot them down, so you can get them answered to your complete satisfaction.

_____

_____

_____

_____

_____

_____

_____

_____

_____

_____

_____

_____

_____

_____

_____

_____

_____

_____

_____

There's something quite powerful to the notion that you can always do things better. I've always focused on that. You can always raise the bar.
—SYLVESTER GREEN
    CORPORATE EXECUTIVE

Understanding Your Credit Report

THE BASICS

There are four types of information included.

> **Personal identifying information:** This includes your name, current and past addresses, Social Security number, date of birth, and employers, past and present.

> **Credit information:** This includes detailed records of your credit accounts, credit cards, and loans. Late payments, skipped payments, accounts turned over to collection agencies, and repossessions appear here as well.

> **Public records:** These are any financial disputes that have involved the court system, including bankruptcy records, tax liens, court judgments against you, and overdue child support.

> **Inquiries:** This lists the names of those who have obtained a copy of your credit report, as well as a record of how many times you have applied for credit in the last two years.

Negative items such as delinquencies, wages garnished, repossessions, court orders, evictions for nonpayment, and missed child support stay on your report for 7 years. Bankruptcy stays on the report for 7 to 10 years, depending on the type of bankruptcy filed for.

Assignment

Study your report carefully. Make sure you can account for everything on it. Mistakes do get made. Look for these common errors:

- Items that you know aren't yours but could belong to someone with the same name or with a similar Social Security number

- Information that is duplicated

- Items that appear past the time that they are required to be kept on your report

If there are negative items that exist as a result of extenuating circumstances, such as an illness or unemployment, write an explanation for the incident and have it added to your report.

You have the right to have any information you know to be incorrect removed from your report. If you find any errors, follow the instructions on the report and request to have them corrected. If you have to send information by mail, it's a good idea to keep copies of your letters and send the information by certified mail, with a return receipt requested. A credit reporting company legally has 30 days to respond to your request.

Do you find any potential errors? What are your questions?

Caveat

Be wary of loan consolidators. Some deals look better on the surface than they actually are. In some cases, consolidation may help protect you from having to file bankruptcy, but do not confuse lower monthly payments with actually *saving* money. If you pay less each month, it will take you much longer to pay the loans off and increase the amount of interest you end up paying. Be especially careful of home equity consolidation loans. Bankers can legally seize your home if something goes wrong.

Take some time to reflect on your credit report. What is your overall reaction? Are you surprised? Worried? Satisfied? Describe how you would like your report to read by the end of this journal.

Notes

_____

_____

_____

_____

_____

_____

_____

_____

_____

_____

_____

_____

_____

Being a Smart Consumer

The famed entrepreneur best known as Madame C. J. Walker became the twenty-first African American to be honored on a commemorative postage stamp in 1998. She is widely referred to as the first African American millionairess (at the time of her death, she was actually worth about $600,000, but that amounts to $6 million today), having amassed her fortune selling hair-care products targeted to the African American community.

Born to ex-slaves as Sarah Breedlove, she was orphaned at age seven and became a child field laborer. She worked as a laundress as a young woman, before founding her own business creating products and training saleswomen in her hair-care methods. As an entrepreneur, Walker was not only targeting an African American consumer, but employing and training thousands of African American women who would otherwise be limited to such professions as laborers or maids.

Before her death in 1919, Walker began organizing her now economically independent workforce into local clubs, which could use their money and clout to improve their communities and protest lynchings and other civil rights abuses. She also worked closely with the NAACP, as well as such visionaries as W.E.B. DuBois and Ida B. Wells-Barnett.

At the height of her success, Walker lived in opulence close to the Rockefellers, but she was also fiercely dedicated to advancing civil rights and helping those less fortunate than herself. "My advice to everyone expecting to go into business," she once said, "is to hit often and to hit hard. In other words, strike with all your might."

Madame C. J. Walker certainly did strike with all her might, and she put her strength and convictions toward the causes she believed in. This month, we're going to examine your point of view as a consumer. We tell the story behind Walker's business to inspire you to begin making your own judgments about the companies behind the products you buy. Are these companies enthusiastically targeting and marketing products to you as an African American? Are they training and advancing African Americans in their workforce? Do they display a concern for the greater good of the community where you live and shop?

You might be asking yourself, why does this matter to me and how can *I* make a difference? Start by considering the fact that African Americans account for more than $5 billion a year that is available to the consumer market. Individually your dollar might not seem like much, but collectively it's a different story. Even if you're not aware of this financial force, today's savvy marketers certainly are. Conferences and marketing firms are popping up all over, talking about how to target the African American and urban markets, because they believe these cultures start global trends. Unfortunately, the world's manufacturers and retail outlets are not nearly as discerning.

As consumers, we need to be way more savvy and vigilant in getting value for our dollars that goes beyond surface satisfaction. Targeting African Americans in a marketing campaign is a good start, but it's also important for you as a consumer to look behind the advertising and figure out whether a company supports the overall advancement of African Americans. At the same time, it is important that you do your part as a consumer to support African American entrepreneurs who are following in the tradition of Madame C. J. Walker. We must train ourselves to be not only *conscious* of our purchasing, but *conscientious* about it.

When you buy a product or patronize a business, how much thought do you give to what kind of a business it is and whether it's hurting or helping the African American community? How can you do better?

_____

_____

_____

_____

_____

_____

_____

_____

_____

Now let's shift our focus back to your personal finances. When you vowed to become a knowledgeable and disciplined consumer, you were making the commitment not to be fooled. Being knowledgeable enables you to guard yourself against being fooled by misleading sales or marketing approaches. Being disciplined enables you to not fool yourself!

In this consumer-driven culture, most of us have become experts at convincing ourselves that we "need" countless things. How many times have you heard yourself say something like "I need a new leather jacket," even though you may have two in your closet? As the expression goes, the more you have, the more you need.

Think about the things in your life that you truly couldn't live without. Aside from the bare essentials (shelter, food, clothing, etc.), are these material things or nonmaterial things, such as the support of your family or the reward you feel from a job well done? What's really most important to you?

_____

_____

_____

_____

_____

_____

_____

_____

_____

_____

_____

_____

_____

_____

_____

Now let's talk about brand loyalty. Are you loyal to certain brands or vendors because they provide the best product at the best value, or is it because they represent something—perhaps something you can't quite define—with which you identify yourself or merely want to be identified? In other words, they offer status. Brand experts, the people whose job it is to influence your decision to buy one product over another simply because of the maker or label attached to it, say that brands carry emotional weight and represent lifestyle choices. The truth is, evocative marketing does tap into real emotions. If you're aware of this, you're less likely to be fooled. The next time you're watching a commercial for the first time, read between the lines. Ask yourself, "What is this trying to make me feel, need, or want?"

Why do you buy certain brands? When you make the decision to pay more for a product, is it for emotional reasons or practical reasons?

_____

_____

_____

_____

_____

_____

_____

Keys to smart shopping are patience, research, and a clear head. The International Mass Retail Association reports that half of all sales are impulse purchases. **A smart consumer doesn't make impulse purchases.** Plan ahead. Either know what you will buy before you walk into a store or enter with a vow to only check out what's there and enforce a strict waiting period of a day or a week before making the purchase. Salespeople will pressure you to buy right away. Do your research. You'll hear this phrase over and over again in this journal, and it's because knowledge is power. Ask around, check consumer magazines and web sites, and compare prices and value among stores.

What current shopping habits are hindering your journey to financial freedom? What habits can you develop that will help move you forward?

_____

_____

_____

_____

_____

_____

_____

_____

_____

_____

_____

_____

_____

_____

_____

_____

_____

_____

_____

_____

_____

_____

_____

_____

_____

_____

_____

_____

_____

_____

It's important on this wealth-building journey to look outside of your individual finances and recognize that you are a part of a larger financial community. Where you choose to bank and shop, which utility company you choose—all choices have effects beyond those on your personal bank account. Where are your dollars going? Are you a help or a hindrance to the development of overall African American wealth? This month we are asking you to be a smart consumer, not only for your own personal development but for the development of the African American community.

Week 1: Don't Let Shopping Become a Vice

Give some thought to your behavior as a consumer. Think back on purchases you know you shouldn't have made. Why did you make them?

_____

_____

_____

_____

_____

_____

_____

_____

_____

_____

_____

_____

_____

_____

_____

_____

_____

_____

_____

_____

_____

_____

_____

> We [African Americans] often buy things to make ourselves appear popular when we really should select products that are more affordable. Our need to maintain a particular public image has damaged us economically.
> —LINDA WEATHERSPOON HAITHCOX ENTREPRENEUR

_____

_____

List five mistakes you've made as a consumer that you vow not to make again:

> There is a way to look at the past. Don't hide from it. It will not catch you if you don't repeat it.
> —PEARL BAILEY
>   SINGER AND ACTRESS

1. _____
2. _____
3. _____
4. _____
5. _____

Five Tips for Saving Money When You Shop

1. Become an off-season shopper. Look for winter clothing sales in the spring. Look at ski equipment in the summertime and outdoor lawn furniture in the winter.

2. Visit high-end stores first to get a look at the best-quality items out there. That way, when you're in a bargain or discount store, you can recognize a high-quality item (as well as big savings).

3. Visit Internet sites that compare and assemble prices for you, such as www.mysimon.com.

4. If you're going to make a big purchase you're not sure of, put it on hold and sleep on it for a day or, if you can, even longer.

5. Look out for the bait and switch. Vendors get you into their stores for an advertised low-price item, then the salesperson tries to talk you into the high-priced "better" product. Know what you need and want and you won't get taken.

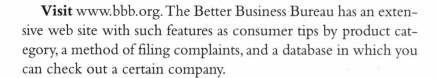

Visit www.bbb.org. The Better Business Bureau has an extensive web site with such features as consumer tips by product category, a method of filing complaints, and a database in which you can check out a certain company.

Assignment

Do a "possessions assessment." Go through your closet, your garage, your storage space. Look around your living room, bedroom, and kitchen. Try to pinpoint your weaknesses as a consumer. For some, it will be buying more than what you need and letting it go to waste. For others, it will be purchasing excessive clothing items, such as numerous pairs of dress shoes you never actually wear. For still others it may be "toys"—electronic gadgets you just *had* to have and now never use.

What do you have a particular weakness for? Explore where that weakness might stem from, and consider specific ways you can control it from now on.

_____

_____

_____

_____

_____

_____

_____

_____

_____

_____

_____

_____

_____

_____

Are Warranties Always the Right Choice?

When a salesperson offers you an extended warranty on a product, think twice. Experts say that most people never use the extended warranty. This is especially true for long-lived, easily maintained appliances like dishwashers and refrigerators. If you do purchase an extended warranty, it should never cost more than 10 percent of what you paid for the product.

Week 2: Getting Smart

Assignment

> Money is sharper than a sword.
> —African proverb

Plan your shopping ahead of time. Get in the habit of making a weekly shopping list for big purchases and start keeping a longer-term wish list. Think about the major purchases you want and need to make. Then research them. For example, if you've got your eye on a gas grill, track prices. Check the Sunday paper, look on the Internet, and do some browsing in stores. Then research brands by reading up on them in consumer magazines. Don't forget to ask your friends and family for their advice. Become more aware of how you spend money and how you plan.

Describe your current planning habits here. Then describe how you will improve them.

_____

_____

_____

_____

_____

_____

_____

_____

Tips for Shopping Smart from Your Home and Avoiding Fraud

The most common problems you might encounter when shopping on the phone, online, or by mail order are delayed delivery, out-of-stock items, incorrect items shipped, damaged items received, and price changes. To avoid these problems:

- **Know who you are dealing with.** If the company isn't familiar to you, check it out with your local or state consumer protection agency.

- **Keep records.** Write down the company name, mailing address, web site, or e-mail address, phone number, description of what you ordered, date, amount you paid, how you paid (check, money order, charge, etc.), and how you delivered your payment (mail, courier service, provided credit card number on phone or online, etc.).

- **Note the delivery period.** Keep any advertisements or materials that show a specific delivery time, or write the delivery time in your records if one was promised.

- **Keep track of your order.** If it's late, it is your choice whether to wait longer or cancel. If you cancel, your money must be refunded within seven days (or your account must be credited within one billing cycle if you charged the order). The company can't substitute a merchandise credit for a refund.

- **Get what you paid for.** When you use a credit card to pay for products or services, you have a right to dispute the charges if the items were not delivered or were misrepresented.

- **Never send cash**—you won't have any proof of payment.

- **Be careful what information you provide.** Give your credit card, debit card, or bank account number only if you're paying for a purchase using that account—never to verify your identity. Don't provide your Social Security number unless you're applying for credit or employment.

Using your personal information, crooks can steal from you and impersonate you to steal from others.

- **Do not do business with an unfamiliar company** whose only address is a post office box. The company may be nothing but a mail drop that will give you little or nothing for your money and will be difficult or impossible to locate if you later have a complaint.

- **Be wary of requests to send your payment by private courier or wire service.** The company may be trying to avoid detection by postal inspectors or to get your money before you have a chance to change your mind.

- **Do not be taken in by lotteries, pyramid schemes, multilevel marketing schemes, or companies that ask for payment in advance,** especially for employment referrals, credit repair, or providing a loan or credit card.

- **Walk away or hang up when you hear the following:** "Sign now or the price will increase," "You have been specially selected . . . ," "You have won . . . ," "All we need is your credit card (or bank account) number—for identification only," "All you pay for is postage, handling, taxes . . . ," "Make money in your spare time—guaranteed income . . . ," "We really need you to buy magazines (a water purifier, a vacation package, office products) from us because we can earn 15 extra credits . . . ," "I just happen to have some leftover material from a job down the street . . . ," "Be your own boss! Never work for anyone else again. Just send in $50 for your supplies and . . . ," "A new car! A trip to Hawaii! $2,500 in cash! Yours, absolutely free! Take a look at our . . . ," "Your special claim number entitles you to join our sweepstakes . . . ," or "We just happen to be in your area and have toner for your copy machine at a reduced price."

From the Federal Consumer Information Center Consumer Action web site.

> Never be afraid to sit a
> while and think.
> —LORRAINE HANSBERRY
>   PLAYWRIGHT

Is your life cluttered with "things"? Give some thought to how much of your time and income you put toward purchasing and maintaining products you could certainly live without.

_____

_____

_____

_____

_____

_____

_____

_____

_____

_____

_____

Bargaining Power

Not every price is set. Have you ever gone into an antiques store or art gallery and bargained back and forth with the owner? Often, it's the smart thing to do. Generally speaking, you should usually be able to negotiate the price on major appliances, vehicles, and consumer electronics equipment. You can also bargain on the extras, such as delivery and installation charges, to reduce a final price. You won't have as much luck bargaining in department stores, discount stores, and catalog showrooms. But the more expensive and widely available a product is, the more likely you'll be able to strike a deal. Some people refuse to bargain for fear of seeming cheap. The truth is, you've nothing to lose and savings to gain, so negotiating a price, in effect, makes you look smart!

from Black Enterprise, *July 1999*

Do individual efforts make a difference where corporate reciprocity is concerned?

"I think my input had an impact," responds Larry Phillips, a network director at the National Aeronautics and Space Administration (NASA) in Greenbelt, Maryland.

"For years, Today's Man in the Rockville [Maryland] store didn't have what I considered an adequate number of African American employees," explains Phillips. Periodically he visited the store to voice his concern to management. "I told them I want to spend money in this store, but I'll wait until I see more African Americans working here."

Now the store not only boasts more African American salespeople, it also has a minority as the store's manager. Phillips is so pleased with the retailer's progress, he will even delay a purchase and wait until the store gets an item in. "I want that store's manager to get credit for the sale," he declares. "Unless we start sponsoring ourselves, we are never going to get anywhere."

Week 3: Doing Your Part

Assignment

Take a lesson from Larry Phillips. This week when you shop, take a closer look at the establishment. Are there African Americans working there? In what kinds of positions? Who owns the establishment? If you're not getting the answers you want to hear, let the store know. If you don't get a positive response, investigate whether there might be a similar store you could patronize that has more African American representation. Remember, your dollar does make a difference and so does speaking your mind.

> We insist that corporations stop the formula of targeting us for consumption and then boycotting us. We don't want to be boycott partners. We want to be trading partners.
> —REV. JESSE L. JACKSON SR.
> CIVIL RIGHTS LEADER

Visit the National Consumer League at www.nclnet.org. This nonprofit organization identifies, protects, represents, and advances the economic and social interests of consumers and workers. The nation's oldest consumer organization, NCL provides government, businesses, and other organizations with the consumer's perspective on concerns including child labor, privacy, food safety, and medication.

> We are one, our cause is one, and we must help each other, if we are to succeed.
> —FREDERICK DOUGLASS
> ABOLITIONIST AND ORATOR

Try to remember a time when you needed support and received it. Did it come from someone in your family? Your church? Your community? From someone who believed in you? Now give some thought to what it means to you to support African American—owned enterprises.

The NAACP's Economic Reciprocity Initiative (ERI) includes the public service of Consumer Choice Guides and Report Cards (visit www.naacp.org), which measure companies in different sectors and give grades that consumers can use as guidelines. For example, in the banking industry, financial services providers were judged in five categories: employment of African Americans, community reinvestment, advertising and marketing, vendor development, and charitable giving. In 1999, Bank of America scored the highest grade, with a B, followed by First Union (C+), Chase Manhattan (C), and Wachovia Corporation (C). The big loser of the group was Sun Trust, with a failing F. Also scoring low were Wells Fargo (D) and Citigroup/Citibank (D).

Assignment

Visit www.naacp.org or contact your local chapter to get the latest Report Cards and advice. Talk to your friends who work at various companies about what those businesses really stand for internally, and when you read black-owned newspapers and magazines or listen to black radio, note the companies that advertise there. Start now to become a knowledgeable and discriminating consumer.

Jot down some questions or interesting discoveries here.

_____

_____

_____

_____

_____

_____

_____

_____

_____

_____

_____

_____

_____

_____

_____

_____

_____

_____

_____

_____

_____

I am overwhelmed by the grace and persistence of my people.
—MAYA ANGELOU
WRITER, POET, AND ORATOR

Know Your Rights

The Community Reinvestment Act (CRA) requires each federal bank regulatory agency to assess how well federally insured institutions meet the needs of their community on the basis of financial conditions and business strategies, competition, and community demographics. You have the right to this information when you make decisions about which bank to use. Visit www.fdic.gov for the ratings of each financial institution that has been evaluated.

Buying a New Car

Studies have shown that African Americans are consistently quoted higher prices for cars by car salespeople, and that women especially are treated less fairly. According to one study conducted nationwide, blacks paid twice the markup that whites did, at a cost of more than $150 million in a year. Don't let this happen to you. Here are some tips for buying a new car:

- Know what you want and what you won't accept *before you walk in the door.* Ignorance is not bliss, it's broke.

- Comparison shop for sticker prices. Do your research before you arrive. Check out www.autoweb.com, www.autovantage.com, www.carpoint.com, and www.autobytel.com to get quotes online. Ask other people how much they paid for the car you're interested in buying.

- Comparison shop for financing as well. Shop in advance for the best deal from your bank or credit union, then compare that information with what is offered you.

- Bring a calculator with you to the dealer. Don't trust the barrage of figures being thrown at you. Determine the total cost, not just the monthly payments.

- The salesperson's goal is to get you to leave that day having bought a car. This is a huge purchase—don't allow yourself to be pressured into a rash purchase.

- Avoid costly unnecessary extras such as credit insurance (this is not required for getting a loan), extended service contracts, auto club memberships, and rustproofing or upholstery finishes.

> If you have to leave your community to take advantage of a special price or sale, then that means your community is not valued by that corporation and your dollars are taken for granted.
>
> —LINDA WEATHERSPOON HAITHCOX
> ENTREPRENEUR

- Carefully read the Buyer's Guide that will be displayed on the car's window.

- Ask for a written price quote before you negotiate trade-ins or financing.

- Don't take possession of the car until all paperwork is final.

- If you have a bad experience with a dealer, contact the Better Business Bureau.

Considering leasing a car? Here are the pros and cons.

Pro: Monthly payments are lower because you only pay for the amount of time you use the car plus interest.

Con: You pay for excessive wear and tear as defined by the lessor. Don't think a ding or a scratch is minor. At lease end, you may have to pay for those repairs.

Pro: You can drive a new car every two to four years.

Con: The car must come back to the lessor in its original condition or you pay to restore it. You may want a better-quality stereo system, for example, but you will pay to replace the old one at lease end.

Pro: Since the monthly payments are lower, you can get more car for your money.

Con: The lessor owns the car, unless the lessee options to buy it at the end-of-term or refinances the remaining amount.

Pro: Most leases require little or no down payment.

Con: The lessee still has to pay for maintenance, traffic tickets, and insurance. Some consumers are under the false impression that the leasing company pays for insurance.

Pro: When the lease ends, you can simply pay any charges, turn the car in, and walk away.

Con: You usually have to carry the highest amount of car insurance.

From *Black Enterprise,* April 2000.

Have you ever had an experience when you felt you were being discriminated against as a consumer or when you disapproved—for any other reason—of the way a proprietor ran his or her business? What did you do about it? What should *you do in the future?*

_____

_____

_____

_____

_____

_____

_____

_____

Remind yourself why your consumer dollars do make a difference.

_____

_____

_____

_____

_____

_____

_____

_____

Getting into the Game of Investing

"If you want success," says renowned attorney Johnnie **Cochran Jr.,** "it's never enough to *know* what you're capable of, you have to *show* what you're capable of. You've got to get into the game in order to demonstrate what you can do."

Cochran was the first African American assistant district attorney of Los Angeles County. He spends his life "in the game." Aside from the high-profile O.J. Simpson case, Cochran has made history with police brutality cases and a myriad of other important verdicts. One of his victories resulted in outlawing the use of the chokehold (which often proved fatal) by Los Angeles police officers. He has served a multitude of high-profile clients, and his autobiography, *Journey to Justice,* was a national best-seller.

Cochran has been actively involved in the causes he is passionate about outside the courtroom as well. He and his wife, Dale, received the prestigious Golden Bell Award, established to honor those who have made a significant contribution toward the improvement of the human condition in the community.

In his personal finances, Cochran has taken his own advice and become an active player in investing. Recently, he took a greater interest in how his money was being managed. In an interview for *Black Enterprise* magazine, Cochran says, "Once I moved to New York, I started spending time with Earl Graves [the publisher of

Black Enterprise] and I began to see how one can live and should live. He's been a resource for me, and I give him a lot of credit for where I am in my planning. Even though I don't plan to retire anytime soon, I do have an exit strategy in place so that I know my wife, children, and law firm will be taken care of."

Cochran offers this advice for those looking to invest: "Get good people who give good advice over a period of time. Then look back and see how you did over the year. You just can't throw [your money] in something and leave it there. You have to review the stuff yourself and make a change when you see fit."

This is an exciting chapter. Today you vow to become a key player in the game of investing. You will no longer stand on the sidelines and watch other people grow their money, yet you will be shrewd about assessing risk. There are three important lessons we can glean from Cochran that apply to this chapter.

1. You can't win if you're not in the game.

2. Seek advice from the experts.

3. Continually reassess your finances.

It takes a wise person to seek and use good advice properly. No one can be an expert on everything, and one of the most important lessons we hope you will take away from this journal is that successful people look for and implement advice from the experts. No matter how successful or how old you are, if you want to continue to grow, you must continue to learn.

Here's the truth about African Americans and personal finance. We continue to make great strides toward narrowing the income gap between blacks and whites. The emergence of our growing middle class, increased opportunities in education, and more and more black role models in positions of authority have all contributed to this progress. But, according to a recent Census Bureau study, the median net worth of black Americans was a devastating one-tenth that of white Americans. Furthermore, even in the income range where the net worth gap is the smallest—

households with income of $50,000 per year and up—black households still possessed only half the wealth of white households. We *must* do better.

One of the greatest contributing factors to these disheartening statistics is the gap between African Americans and white Americans when it comes to investing. A 1998 study sponsored by Ariel Mutual Funds (a black-owned investment firm) and Charles Schwab & Company showed that 57 percent of African Americans polled said they owned stock, compared to 81 percent of white Americans polled. When asked whether they had brokerage or mutual fund accounts, 56 percent of African Americans answered yes and 71 percent of whites answered yes. A 2000 study showed that the percentage of black stock market investors earning $50,000 or more per year rose from 57 percent in 1997 to 64 percent in 1999. The percentage of whites in the same income group hovered at just about 80 percent. Though the number of people in our community who choose to invest is growing, it's not growing nearly fast enough.

Simply put, we are making money, we are saving money, but we are not *investing* our money the way we should be. All the experts agree: True wealth accumulation takes more than saving. You must invest your money to see it grow. The average return on company stocks will double your money in six to seven years. No savings account will do that for you. At the very least, investing helps protect your savings from inflation. For example, if the inflation rate is 3 percent (an average figure) and your savings account is earning you only 2 percent, you're losing money. Over time, you will see the compounding value of investments. For example, if you contribute $100 a month to an investment vehicle with an average annual return of 18 percent, in 10 years you'll have $33,625. In 20 years you'll have $234,349.

The 2000 Ariel-Schwab study pointed to several different hypothesized factors to explain why African Americans are less likely to invest: less of a family history of investing, single-parent families, individuals who are financially supporting extended family members, and a cultural mistrust of the stock market.

Do you invest your money? If not, why not? Did your parents or grandparents? What preconceived notions or biases do you hold, if any, about investing? What are your reservations about investing your money?

_____

_____

_____

_____

_____

_____

_____

_____

_____

_____

_____

_____

_____

_____

_____

_____

_____

_____

_____

_____

The first order of business is to determine your risk factor. Depending on your age, your financial goals and how much money you put away, you can decide what percentage of your savings you can invest in the stock market. As you begin to research this area you will hear the call, "Diversify! diversify! diversify!" This refers to several basic strategies for spreading your investments out, all of which are designed to safeguard your money while providing you with the opportunity to seize wealth.

The first way you diversify is to put your investment money in a mix of high-, medium-, and low-risk venues. These three elements make up your portfolio.

If you're asking, what exactly is a **portfolio,** the answer is straightforward. It's a combination of stocks or company shares (which provide the fastest growth), bonds for stable but more modest earnings, and cash to safeguard against unexpected losses and to help you take advantage of investment opportunities. **Asset allocation** is simply how you divide your money (your assets) among these three areas. Your allocation is dictated by how much risk you can afford to take (not to mention your stomach for gambling).

Dividends are portions of the company's profit paid to a shareholder. In some cases, dividends can become lucrative, but generally speaking money is made from buying a stock and subsequently selling it at a higher price. Owning stocks can be accomplished in two basic ways: You can pick a company and buy individual shares from it or you can join a mutual fund by pooling your investments with other investors and spreading out your shares among a collection of investments. This is another way to diversify. The more companies you are invested in, the less one company's losses can effect you. **Mutual funds** fall into two categories: tax-deferred (such as a 401(k) or IRA fund) and taxable (earnings you'll use before retirement). But remember, the reverse is also true—the great success of one company will be leveled by the lesser performers in the group. Buying shares offers the chance of a better, more dramatic payoff but also has higher risks.

Remember, there are many different types of mutual funds to choose from. You are trusting the fund and the fund manager with your hard-earned money. Think of it as being similar to hiring a key coworker. What would you investigate when hiring someone? Find out about their credentials and past performance, their goals for the future, and whether their personality is compatible with yours.

Look for **no-load** funds—that is, funds that impose no sales charge, or load, on their investors for membership. Investors buy shares directly from a fund company instead of from a broker. This is a great safeguard against the old complaint against brokers who convince their clients to buy a stock because he or she gets paid on commission by the number of trades made, regardless of the financial outcome for the client. However, watch out for funds with high sales commissions and fees.

Bonds are debts issued for a period of more than one year. When you buy a bond, you're essentially lending your money. The seller (the government or a private company) agrees to repay the principal amount of the loan, plus interest, at a specified time. Interest-bearing bonds pay interest periodically in the form of coupons. Bonds provide stable, predictable, *fixed* income, if you wait until the bond matures to cash it in.

Last, cash on hand (usually in the form of bank accounts, money market funds, CDs, or Treasury bills) in your portfolio allows you to make up for an unexpected loss or to dive into a unexpected opportunity. This cash is not to be confused with your emergency savings fund. If you're a beginner, remember, it takes time to build a portfolio. Don't be discouraged if you don't have the funds available just yet. With perseverance, you will.

Generally speaking, you don't need to worry about timing the market. Being consistent in your contributions and following some basic guidelines will pay off over time. A smart strategy is **dollar-cost averaging,** when you automatically transfer the same amount of your money into your investments each month, guaranteeing that you will buy fewer shares when the price is high and more shares when the price is low. Studies have shown that consistently investing over the long term (instead hopping in and out when the market fluctuates) is a sure way to build wealth. For example, if you were to present a one-year-old with a trust of $1,000 today and keep that money invested, never adding to it, it would be worth almost $1 million when that child turns 60.

With the popularity of the Internet, crucial information— information that used to be available only to professional investors—is now available to amateurs. In their best-selling book *The Motley Fool Investment Guide,* brothers David and Tom Gardner harness the power of communication and information sharing that takes place on their web site (www.fool.com) to beat out Wall Street's "wise men" at their own game by cutting out the intermediary. The Gardners advise against conventional wisdom and the new tradition of mutual funds, as well as the belief that the broker always knows best. The "fools" as they refer to themselves, argue that we are all capable of evaluating companies and making wise decisions about our own money.

It's a question of choice. If you're a high-stakes personality, you may get frustrated by a conservative, long-term plan. If taking risks makes you nervous and you don't have a lot to lose, you would be better paired with a conservative strategy. In this chapter, we'll take a closer look at all of the elements involved and the choices available to you.

What's most important is your commitment to learning about investing, no matter how much or how little you already know, as well as your commitment to get into investing for the long haul. So be patient. Whichever direction you decide to take with your investments, we encourage you to dig deeper. Read books on the subject. The *Black Enterprise Guide to Investing* by James Anderson is a great place to start. Take a class on investing. Start or join an investment club. Faithfully keep up with financial journals and web sites. There is no doubt that we can change the statistics about African Americans and the stock market, one person at a time, by getting into the game! Most important for you personally, by consistently investing, you can change the course of your life.

Week 1: The Basics

Assignment

Pick a Stock

Getting started is simple. Pick a stock and follow it. If you don't already know how, learn how to read the stock tables by referring to the guide that follows. Choose a company that means something to you—a company or product you know and believe in. Follow its progress, up or down. Find out if the company is making profits (a good pick is making at least 10 percent in profits each year) and what its debt status is (does it have more debt than cash?). Investigate the company. Scour its web site. Read about its industry in the *Wall Street Journal* and other financial publications. Follow how factors such as inflation, management changes, or economic events affect the stock. Record your findings here.

Pick up the *New York Times* and follow the activity of the New York Stock Exchange, using the following guide. Get in the habit of checking the stock market in the *Times* or the *Wall Street Journal* for the stocks you may own or those you'd like to own.

52 Weeks   The 52-week high and low shows the price range in which the stock has traded over the previous 52-week period.

Stock   Name of the company

Sym   The stock symbol indicates the letters used to identify companies listed on the exchange which they trade.

Div   The cash dividend per share indicates an estimate of the anticipated annual dividend per share in dollars and cents.

Yld   The yield is the percentage rate of return paid on a stock in dividends.

PE   The price-to-earnings (P/E) ratio tells you the relationship between the stock's price and earnings per share.

Vol   The volume column shows you how many stocks were sold on a given day.

Hi Lo   The high and low columns show a stock's trading range for the day.

Close   The close column shows what a stock's price was at the end of the day.

Net Chg   The net change column compares the day's closing price with that of the day before.

Keeping Track

An index tracks a group of stocks. You can use these to judge how a stock or mutual fund is performing in comparison to the rest of the market. Indexes are also referred to as **benchmarks.** You hear them all the time on the news, but do you really know what the following indexes stand for?

- **Dow Jones Industrial Average (the Dow):** Performance measure of 30 top stocks (usually **blue-chip stocks,** or the largest, most successful U.S. companies) that trade on the New York Stock Exchange.

- **Standard & Poor's 500 (S&P 500):** A measure of the performance of 500 of the largest companies (**large cap,** or large capitalization; **capitalization** = number of a company's shares × stock price). Compiled by the research firm Standard & Poor's.

- **Nasdaq Composite (the National Association of Securities Dealers Automated Quotations):** A measure of about 4,000 technology stocks. These stocks are traded in an over-the-counter (**OTC**) market—a decentralized market where geographically dispersed dealers are linked together by telephones and computer screens, *as opposed to on the market floor.*

- There are many others, such as the **MSCI EAFE** (the Morgan Stanley Capital International, Europe, Australia, and the Far East) and the **Russell 2000,** an index of small-cap stocks. Familiarize yourself with them. Visit www.bloomberg.com or www.dailystock.com for comprehensive listings.

Confused by all the jargon? Visit www.money.com and check out Money 101. The site has a glossary of over 2,500 financial terms.

THE RULE OF 72

To find out how long it will take for an investment to double your money, divide the number 72 by the compound annual rate (use a whole number) of your investment.

Think about the concept of doubling your hard-earned money. Return to some of the financial goals you set for yourself at the beginning of this journal. Does the prospect of investing make those goals more tangible?

Four Basic Categories of Mutual Funds

There are four basic categories of mutual funds.

- **Money market funds:** Municipal money market funds invest in local and state government debt and are tax free.
- **Bond funds:** Types include U.S. government bonds, corporate bonds, and municipal bonds.
- **Stock funds:** Categories include sector funds, international funds, and small-, mid-, and large-cap funds.
- **Balanced funds:** These are a combination of the other three.

Asset allocation funds move asset percentages around among the different types of investments to optimize portfolio performance. This makes for a higher-risk balanced fund.

Choosing a Stock Mutual Fund

A stock mutual fund or equity fund is a good choice if its returns have exceeded 12 percent on a regular basis. Generally, 10 to 12 percent is considered a moderately good fund. Anything below 9 percent is a bad choice.

Actively Managed Funds versus Index Funds

Actively managed funds seek to beat out the index performances, whereas index funds seek to match the index performance by literally buying each of the funds indexed. Keep in mind that actively managed funds make more trades, thereby incurring a higher capital gains tax, which *you,* as the investor, pay for. When judging the profitability of a mutual fund, be sure to look at its **tax-adjusted returns**—that is, the money the fund makes after you pay the capital gains tax.

Mutual Funds' Best-Kept Secret

Interestingly, the Gardners assert in *The Motley Fool Investment Guide* that 75 percent of mutual funds underperform the market's average return each year. For that reason, they recommend an index fund such as Vanguard's Index Trust 500 Portfolio, a multi-billion-dollar fund that invests in all of the S&P 500 stocks, therefore matching the S&P's performance. **Why don't you hear about index funds from most financial planners or see them advertised on television?** The fools wisely point out that financial planners don't put money into their own pockets when their clients invest in index funds. Index funds, because they simply invest in everything in the index, don't hire experts to make judgments about which stocks to choose. Index funds also don't sink a lot of money into advertising. How do you invest in an index fund? Try a discount or online broker. Visit www.gomez.com for advice about online and discount brokers.

Visit www.morningstar.com for mutual fund ratings and a boatload of investing advice and research.

Assignment

Investigate the many choices out there for mutual funds. (Visit www.fool.com for more on the Motley Fool's advice.) This will involve some research online and in financial publications.

Take your time, and keep track of the results here.

_____

_____

_____

Now, do a little analysis. Outline the pros and cons of your top picks.

Check out the **Black Enterprise Black Stock and Fund Index.** Visit www.blackenterprise.com for listings of the top black-owned companies and mutual funds.

THE 100 PERCENT RULE

Subtract your age from 100 percent to determine how much of your money you can allocate to aggressive investments. Of course, this is just a rough estimate, but it gives you a general idea of how much stability you need and it also gets you started.

Assignment

Determine your risk factor. Investigate by doing some research online or visit a financial planner to determine how best to allocate your assets. The two most important factors are time and the amount of money you can afford to lose. Questions to keep in mind: What do you plan to use your earnings for? When do you expect to use the earnings? How essential are they? For example, are you saving to buy a new boat or for your child's college education?

_____

_____

_____

_____

_____

_____

_____

If you have only a small amount of money to invest and you are young, you have the ingredients essential to becoming financially independent," says Cheryl D. Broussard, financial advisor and author of *The Black Woman's Guide to Financial Independence.* Were you to invest roughly $100 a month starting today, you would amass $1 million in 45 years, assuming a return of 12%. (Over the past 20 years, the average annual rate for the S&P 500 stock index was 17.9%.)
—*BLACK ENTERPRISE,* MARCH 2000

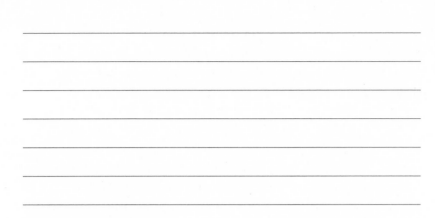

Who Is Mr. Market?

And why should he matter to you? Mr. Market is a character that Benjamin Graham, the legendary investor, made up to personify pricing in the stock market. In his book *The Intelligent Investor,* written in 1949, Graham says, "Sometimes his idea of value appears plausible and justified by business developments and prospects as you know them. Often, on the other hand, Mr. Market lets his enthusiasm or his fears run away with him, and the value he proposes seems to you a little short of silly."

A perfect example of Mr. Market getting carried away was the overvaluing of certain high-tech stocks when the Internet boom hit. These companies had stocks that were trading at outrageous highs, only to end up, in some cases, declaring bankruptcy a few years later. What can you learn from Mr. Market? Stocks are not always priced at what they're worth, and the more you learn, the more you'll be able to take advantage of that fact.

This brings us to the big strategy question: value or growth stocks? What's your style?

Benjamin Graham, along with fellow Columbia Business School professor David Dodd, are the fathers of the school of value investing. **Value investing** is the art of investing in real bargains (stocks that are priced far below their intrinsic value) and then waiting—patiently—for the price of the stock to rise. This is how legendary investor Warren Buffet made his fortune. Value investors look for unpopular, undervalued stocks that have been dropping in price for several years. They buy at rock bottom, only when they decide that the company actually has what it takes to

turn a good profit over time. This strategy goes against the conventional wisdom of the hour, as well as the whim of Mr. Market. Value investing consistently outperforms growth investing, but over long periods of time.

"Over time" is the key phrase here. **Growth stocks** are associated with high risk but, when you're lucky, big and faster returns. A growth manager looks for a company with rapidly growing earnings, which he or she banks on earning even more. This strategy follows momentum in the marketplace and looks for the hottest stocks. Most portfolios employ a combination of the two investing strategies.

What's your philosophy? If you don't have one yet (and that's just fine), start to formulate some ideas toward a philosophy.

_____

_____

_____

_____

_____

_____

_____

_____

_____

_____

_____

_____

_____

_____

> My basic philosophy in investing is I buy and hold, sort of like that Warren Buffett guy. But I am willing to change if I see there's going to be some problems. . . . You can't be too attached to your stocks and your portfolio. You have to be able to let go if it's going to hurt your overall financial picture.
> —KENDALL GILL
>   NBA ATHLETE

Diversify!

Invest internationally. International mutual funds let you participate in the growth of foreign economies. Diversifying around the world is one way to reduce investment risk. Investing across different industries is another way to diversify.

Week 4: Trust the Experts or Go It Alone?

This is it. We've been through "ready, set"—now it's time to go! Some people find it best to trust their investments to the experts. Financial services companies such as Vanguard, T. Rowe Price, and TIAA-CREF offer low fees and good customer service.

Some of you may decide to take matters into your own hands, either privately or as part of an investment club. Your choice should come after examining whether you have the time, knowledge, and, frankly, the desire to go it alone.

Do you think you'd have fun investing your own money? Are you willing to put the necessary time into the process? Or would you rather put your research efforts toward finding the right advisor?

_____

_____

_____

_____

_____

_____

_____

_____

_____

_____

_____

_____

_____

_____

The **Coalition of Black Investors** (cobinvest.com) is a great resource for a variety of investment needs.

Start an investment club. Check out *The Millionaire's Club* by Carolyn M. Brown or contact the National Organization of Investors Corporation.

If you only have a small amount to invest, consider **discount brokers** that simply invest your money where you ask them to. You get no advice, but you don't pay for advice either! Or, for as little as $50 a month, you can invest in a **dividend reinvestment plan** (DRIP) where you buy stocks directly from a company. This is usually called the company's **direct purchase program.**

Blackenterprise.com's **ShareBuilder** gives investors a new and unique way to invest for the long term. Through Share-Builder, you can set up an account entirely online that will build your portfolio over time, by making automatic, recurring dollar-based investments. ShareBuilder offers an affordable avenue for investors to build a portfolio of stocks and emphasizes the accumulation of stock rather than trading.

Visit *Black Enterprise*'s **Direct Stock Purchase Center** to purchase equities directly from companies—without brokerage fees. You can choose from more than 1,500 high-quality stocks in sectors ranging from manufacturing and energy to technology and telecommunications.

from Black Enterprise, *January 2001*

Jasmine Guy, formerly of the hit television series *A Different World* and the Broadway play *Chicago,* has been drawn to the stock market in recent years. Formerly, her financial strategy was conservative. She had moderate success in real estate. The rest of her money went into CDs and a few corporate bonds. "Looking back, I wish I had been in the market because the nineties was a great time to be in it—even if I'd taken what I spent on shoes," says Guy.

Her newfound respect for the stock market was nurtured in 1997 after she met her husband, Terrence M. Duckette, a broker with A.G. Edwards & Sons, a St. Louis–based financial firm. Duckette helped Guy implement a new approach. "I think he was shocked at how little interest my money had been accruing over the previous 10 years," says Guy. "But my argument to him was, 'At least the money ain't gone.'"

Duckette, an investment veteran with more than a decade's worth of experience, says "I understand that, with actors, they'll have periods when they'll have chunks of money coming in and you have to be conservative, but a 3 percent checking account or CD is not going to cut it."

Duckette advised Guy to delve into blue-chip stocks, international equities, and sector plays with strong long-term potential, such as pharmaceuticals. He also had Guy invest in some of the solid companies that sell products she uses every day, such as FedEx Corp. (NYSE: FDX) and Boeing (NYSE: BA). In fact, Guy scored with her selection of Philip Morris (NYSE: MO). "[It] was a good pick," says Duckette, whose wife suggested they invest in the tobacco giant at the height of the negative fallout impacting it. "People don't realize that Philip Morris also owns Kraft Foods and Miller Brewing, so it's not just a tobacco company."

For Guy, acquiring new knowledge about investing has become part of her routine. She also understands that her financial decisions will directly affect her husband and their daughter, Imani. Asserts Guy, "If I take $20,000 out, that's $20,000 that's not going to make the 10 percent or 20 percent it could make in the market."

We may not all have $20,000 to invest, but we can all learn something from Jasmine Guy's story. Think about your own finances. Do you have money that's not earning what it should be earning? Do you need to revamp a policy that may be too conservative or not conservative enough?

_____

_____

_____

_____

_____

_____

_____

_____

_____

_____

_____

_____

_____

_____

_____

_____

_____

_____

_____

Assignment

Begin. Start the ball rolling. Invest now. If you've never invested, start out by putting the majority of your investment money in funds and bonds, but do try your hand at picking a stock and investing, a little at a time. If you're already investing, explore how you can branch out or up the ante a bit.

Notes

_____

_____

_____

_____

_____

_____

_____

_____

_____

_____

_____

_____

_____

_____

_____

_____

_____

_____

_____

_____

_____

_____

_____

_____

_____

_____

_____

_____

_____

_____

_____

_____

_____

_____

_____

_____

_____

_____

_____

Your Midyear Assessment

As president and CEO of Carver Federal Savings Bank, the nation's largest African American–operated bank, located in Harlem, Deborah C. Wright seems to have found a job that was tailor-made just for her. Before coming to Carver, she was president and CEO of the Upper Manhattan Empowerment Zone Development Corporation. There she successfully led the start-up of the nation's largest empowerment zone, managing a $300-million budget of federal, state, and local funding. Her joint business and law degree from Harvard University, along with her previous experience in community development, were also perfectly aligned steps toward her current position. But if it hadn't been for a brave and dramatic about-face in her career several years back, Wright might very well be in an entirely different position today.

When Wright graduated from Harvard she went into investment banking. "When I look back on it," she says, "I didn't really make a choice. I went with the herd." Though she worked for a prominent investment firm and was financially very successful, she says she felt hollow inside. At that point she did something she never imagined herself doing: She quit her job without another prospect and began a period of searching for a career that would make her happy.

She found it. Though she was earning less than half of her

previous income, Wright was thrilled to start a job for the New York Partnership and begin her career in community development. "It was one of the best years of my life because I felt what I was doing mattered to somebody." From there Wright's career blossomed, and she landed a position as commissioner of the New York City Department of Housing Preservation and Development. Of her search for the right path, Wright says, "I had come to realize that I wasn't looking for a job, I was looking for a mission."

We chose Deborah Wright's inspiring story for this chapter, your midyear review, to illustrate an important point: Sometimes changing horses in midstream is absolutely the right choice. This chapter is about **assessment**—looking back and looking forward on your wealth-building journey—and we want you to be open to change and improvement. Just because you've gone about this process in a certain way over the last five months doesn't mean that you have to continue in the exact same fashion. Unless, of course, you're already feeling successful.

Congratulations! You've completed the real meat and potatoes of the wealth-building initiative: You've worked on straightening out your current finances; you've become a smarter consumer; you've vowed to set aside savings; and you've delved into the important task of investing. If you feel these congratulations aren't entirely due, don't worry. Over the next month, one of your assignments will be to go back over what you were supposed to do (and no doubt had every intention of doing) but somehow didn't entirely accomplish. Now is the time to repair your mistakes.

Now is also the time to look to what you have ahead of you over the next six months—and over your continued course of financial empowerment—and reassess, or perhaps just remind yourself of, your own personal mission.

Have you surprised yourself and accomplished more than you thought you could have, or do you wish you'd accomplished more? Whichever it is, write about your current reflections and gut feelings.

_____

_____

_____

_____

_____

_____

_____

_____

_____

_____

_____

_____

_____

The other part of your job this month is to determine your **net worth.** This is the real thing, the true definition of wealth. Your net worth is not a measure of your income or your possessions; it's the tally of all your current assets—your property, cash, and investments—minus your liabilities, or your debts. If you find you have a *negative* net worth, that means you owe more than you own. For the rest of your financial life, you should determine your success and position by referring to your net worth. Driving an expensive car, having a closet full of designer clothes, or living in a luxury apartment doesn't necessarily mean you will be able to provide for yourself, your family, or future generations—which is the ultimate goal of financial empowerment.

This month, we ask you to pause and take some time to reassess your financial goals. Don't lose track of your mission. And remember: It's never too late to start anew.

Assignment

Admit it. There has to be at least one assignment, one journal entry, or one initiative from the past five months that you haven't completed yet. For you overachievers who are saying, "I've done everything!"—there must be *something* you think you could have done better or more thoroughly. Your assignment for this week is to go back and complete any unfinished tasks.

Review your **monthly budgets.** *Are you keeping up the practice? Have you managed to spend less money as a result of keeping to a budget? Give some thought to reevaluating your spending and your budgeting. How can you do better?*

What about your **debt and credit practices?** *If you had a significant debt, are you chipping away at it successfully? Are you using credit carefully? Again, what are some ways you can further improve your debt and credit practices?*

Week 2: Keeping Organized

Read back through your journal entries. Do you see a change in your approach or attitude toward wealth building? How do you see yourself changing? What changes would you still like to see in yourself?

_____

_____

_____

_____

_____

_____

_____

_____

_____

_____

_____

_____

What is the status of your **emergency savings?** Do you have enough to support yourself and your family for three to six months? If not, set a deadline right now for getting it up to par. Here, make a fair assessment of where you stand with your **retirement savings?**

_____

_____

_____

_____

_____

_____

_____

_____

_____

_____

_____

_____

_____

_____

_____

_____

_____

_____

_____

_____

Assignment

Now that you are investing, you need to make sure you are keeping organized and thorough records. Organize or reorganize your financial papers. Create a filing system that provides easy access to financial documents and records.

Week 3: Determining Your Net Worth

Assignment

Assess Your Net Worth

Complete the following worksheet:

Assets:

Checking account _____

Savings account _____

Savings certificates _____

Savings bonds _____

Market value of home or apartment _____

Market value of other real estate _____

Cash value of life insurance policy _____

Surrender value of annuities _____

Equity in pension or profit-sharing plan _____

IRA and Keogh plans _____

Market value of: _____

    Stocks _____

    Bonds _____

    Mutual funds _____

    Other investments _____

> It doesn't matter how much money you make, or how fancy your clothes and your car are. If you have a lot more money going out than coming in, you are poor!
> —REV. DARRIN MOORE
> AME ZION CHURCH
> PASTOR

Current value of: _____

    Automobiles _____

    Household furnishings and appliances _____

    Furs, jewelry, and other large luxury items _____

    Loans receivable _____

    Any other assets _____

Total assets _____

Liabilities: _____

    Current bills _____

    Mortgage balance _____

    Credit card balances _____

    Auto loans _____

    Student loans _____

    Check overdraft line of credit owed _____

    Home equity loans _____

    Other debts _____

Total liabilities: _____

Subtract liabilities from assets to determine **net worth** _____

Are you pleased with or disappointed by your net worth? Where do you see room for improvement?

_____

_____

_____

_____

_____

_____

_____

_____

_____

_____

_____

What would you like your net worth to be at the end of this year? In five years? In ten years?

_____

_____

_____

_____

_____

_____

_____

Week 4: Looking Forward

Carver Bank CEO Deborah Wright makes the distinction between a *job* and a *mission*. Don't forget to make a distinction between the figures and equations related to wealth building and the ultimate goal—the mission—that drives you.

What's more important to you than simply a bigger bank account? Define your personal mission here.

_____

_____

_____

_____

_____

_____

_____

_____

_____

_____

_____

_____

_____

_____

_____

_____

_____

_____

TIP Do you set aside **time each week to review your finances?** If you don't, start now. If you are married or have children who are old enough to participate, do at least some of it together as a family.

How are you doing on the **financial goals** *you laid out in Chapter 1? Remember visualizing them earlier. Have they changed?*

_____

_____

_____

_____

_____

_____

_____

_____

"The decision to invest or save discretionary income versus consume it is a zero-sum decision. If all of the discretionary income that you decide to consume is not available to invest, then by default you've made a decision not to invest or save," asserts John E. Williams, chair of the department of economics and business at Morehouse College in Atlanta.

"We still have a nation of consumers instead of wealth accumulators. You gain real wealth through a long-term program of savings and investment."

From _Black Enterprise_, April 2000

What kind of **consumer** _are you? Have you improved your shopping habits? What do you still need to work on?_

_____

_____

_____

_____

_____

_____

_____

_____

_____

_____

_____

_____

_____

_____

_____

_____

_____

_____

_____

_____

_____

_____

_____

_____

_____

_____

_____

Success Story

from Black Enterprise, *February 2000*

When Aylwin Lewis, executive vice president of operations and new business for Tricon Global Restaurants, took the summer off from grad school at the University of Washington in Seattle, he did not know that a desire to earn extra money would lead to a career in the fast-food industry, let alone the number-three spot in the largest restaurant company in the world. Some 22 years later, Lewis has gone from being assistant manager at one Jack-in-the-Box in his native Houston to running 29,800 restaurants worldwide for Tricon Global Restaurants Inc., whose chains include Taco Bell, KFC, and Pizza Hut, each the number-one brand in its food category.

After becoming a district manager with Jack-in-the-Box and then managing 40 of its Los Angeles stores, Lewis was lured away by PepsiCo in 1984 to be regional operations manager for a soup-and-salad chain start-up. When the division was sold, Lewis declined an offer to stay with the franchise. In 1987, he was back at Jack-in-the-Box as a regional vice president with 100 stores, valued at $100 million, under his command. He propelled profits in his area's stores from −0.4 to 120 percent over the next six years.

In 1993, PepsiCo offered Lewis the position of regional general manager for KFC, which was followed by a series of promotions, from senior director of franchising to senior vice president of operations development and marketing. In 1997, after PepsiCo spun off its Tricon restaurants division, Lewis was promoted to COO for Pizza Hut. He once again turned around a sluggish but well-known brand, producing nine consecutive quarters of positive growth, aided by his innovative "Operation Boot Camp" strategy, which ensured that employee training was consistent among all 4,000 restaurants. The U.S. Pizza Hut unit grossed $4.8 billion of the corporation's $20.6 billion in sales in 1998. After gaining a 22 percent share of the market, Lewis was rewarded with a promotion to executive vice president of operations and new business for all Tricon restaurants.

Along the way, Lewis also found time to return to his educational goals: He received a master's degree in human resource management from Houston Baptist University and an MBA from the University of Houston, his alma mater. An avid reader who has traveled to almost 50 countries with his wife, Lewis believes in staying hungry and humble, "so the trappings of the job don't go to your head. I come from the Walter Payton school of achievement. I think you do the job until it gets done and let the work speak for itself."

Think back on your own life. Has an unexpected change, like the one Lewis experienced, changed your life? Are you looking for something new? What would you like to see change in your professional and financial life?

Notes

_____

_____

_____

_____

_____

_____

_____

_____

_____

_____

_____

_____

_____

_____

_____

_____

_____

_____

_____

_____

_____

_____

_____

_____

_____

Handling Your Taxes

Why is Bill Cosby's humor so universal? His subject matter, ranging from marriage to raising children to visiting the dentist, speaks to the essence of everyday life. Growing up in a poor Philadelphia neighborhood, Cosby's first audience was his mother, for whom he acted out humorous skits about everyday household happenings. His elementary school friends at the time—among them, Fat Albert and Old Weird Harold—also served as source material for themes that he would later incorporate into his thesis project for his doctorate in education and, of course, a popular children's show.

Cosby never stopped drawing on material from his life as he went on to become a cultural icon and one of the wealthiest people in the entertainment business. For his work on *The Cosby Show,* one of the most influential shows in television's history, *Time* magazine praised Cosby as "dominating the medium as no star has since the days of Lucille Ball and Milton Berle." Coretta Scott King described the show as "the most positive portrayal of a black family that has ever been broadcast." Beginning with his first job on television, as costar of *I Spy* (one of the first instances of a black character being cast alongside a white equal), Cosby has displayed a deep concern for projecting positive images of African Americans in the media.

> You can turn painful situations around through laughter. If you can find humor in anything—even poverty—you can survive it.
> —BILL COSBY
>   ACTOR, COMEDIAN,
>   AND AUTHOR

Cosby's successes are certainly not limited to the screen. One of the best-selling comedians on record, he is also the author of several best-selling books, including *Fatherhood* (Doubleday/Dolphin, 1986), which sold more than 2.6 million copies in hardcover and 1.5 million in paperback. Bill Cosby built an empire from his own unique brand of humor; his financial accomplishments are paramount. In an interview on *Larry King Live* on the Cable News Network (CNN), Larry King said to Cosby, "You don't have to work."

"Yes I do," Cosby answered.

"Why?" King followed up.

"Because I love it," he answered.

King pressed on, saying that Cosby didn't need to work economically, to which he quipped back, "Yeah, but what difference does that make? Did Exxon quit pumping?" On a more serious note, Cosby went on to add, "I enjoy what I'm doing. The thoughts are always turning, churning. And there are things that I want to say."

Cosby is also a stellar example of a person who has shared his success with the African American community. He has put forth tireless effort in the name of education and other charitable causes—notably, a $20-million gift to Spelman College and the establishment of an educational foundation to honor his son, the late Ennis Cosby.

Bill Cosby's story is as unique as it is inspiring, and we hope that it also will remind you of the importance of keeping your sense of humor. His astute ability to create humor out of life's everyday nitty-gritty is something we can all learn from. Laughter is said to reduce stress, relax muscles, and increase endorphins—but most important, it helps you to put things in perspective and not take yourself too seriously. Cosby's story is also a good reminder that money alone, though powerful and well worth pursuing, is not the measure by which we should define our lives.

We thought we'd start this month out on an upbeat note,

because we suspect that most of you *didn't* read the heading of this chapter and think to yourselves, "Great, taxes!" It's become a cliché: People hate doing their taxes. Most people (unless it's their birthday) dread April 15. When most of us conjure up the image of an IRS worker, we imagine a curmudgeonly ogre, ready to snatch up our hard-earned money. So it's very likely you have not been looking forward to this month in your wealth-building journey.

Well, try to adjust your attitude. Start over and pretend the chapter heading reads "Found Money." That is essentially what you stand to gain by becoming a more savvy taxpayer. Furthermore, it's not as complicated as you might think. What about that curmudgeonly character? Actually, through the Internet, the IRS has recently made paying your taxes much more accessible and efficient—yet another good reason to jump on board the tech train. Detailed, easy to understand information is as close as your keyboard. The IRS also holds free tax-preparation clinics, distributes free publications, and will even answer your specific questions over the phone.

Now, about April 15: Aside from the hoopla at your local post office, tax day should be like any other day of the year. First, you sloughed off your procrastinating ways long ago on this journey, so you won't be in line at 11:59! Second—and this is perhaps the most important lesson of the Found Money chapter—the only way to save on your taxes is to think of it as a yearlong task. Whichever day you file, the very next day the process begins all over again. Smart taxpayers know that decisions about investments, education, buying a home, making charitable contributions, and myriad other financial transactions that take place all year long have significant tax-related consequences.

Intrinsic to this point is the need to keep and *organize* all your related receipts and paperwork. There are several tax software programs available that will keep your records in impeccable shape. But a simple filing system works as well. If you're not the type who likes filing, try this approach: Start a financial in-box, or catchall, somewhere at home. Toss the receipts and paperwork in there as soon as you get them. Then, when you are doing your *weekly* financial sweep, organize and file the records all at once. Wait more than a week and it quickly becomes an overwhelming task, so be consistent.

The major strategies for saving money on your taxes are pretty straightforward:

1. Make sure you claim all tax credits you and your family are eligible for.

2. Make sure you have claimed the maximum in deductions you rightfully have coming to you.

3. Be tax-smart when investing.

4. Make sure you seek the appropriate help with filing when needed.

The best way to avoid being audited is to double-check your arithmetic. It may sound outrageously obvious, but arithmetic mistakes caught by IRS computers flag you for potential audits. Generally speaking, being self-employed or earning over $100,000 per year will slightly increase your chances of being audited. Or, if you're paid in cash for your work, as are table servers or dealers in casinos, your chances may also be increased. Doctors seem to get audited a lot, too. If your return stands out for your income bracket (i.e., you earn $40,000 but donated $15,000 to charities), it's more likely that you'll be flagged as well. To help avoid this, if you know of anything that may look unusual, attach receipts or a canceled check to substantiate it, just in case. This can stop further inquiries. Finally, many people are selected to be audited by the pure chance of random selection. You can't control that, but you can be prepared if you hold on to your documentation. The theme for this chapter is **keep records!** And remember to make copies of everything you send to the IRS.

If you decide to get help filing your taxes, be very selective about whom you hire. Interview the person face-to-face, and find out how he or she gets paid—that is, flat fee, hourly rate, or fee based on a percentage of your return.

Week 1: Claiming Tax Credits

What has your relationship with filing taxes been like in the past? Do you dread it? Do you pay someone else to do it? Or is filing your taxes not as torturous for you as it is for others? Take a vow to become as tax-savvy as you can be and to look at the brighter side of taxes.

_____

_____

_____

_____

> Every successful plan begins with having the right attitude.
> —BROOKE STEPHENS
>   FINANCIAL CONSULTANT

_____

_____

_____

_____

_____

_____

_____

_____

_____

_____

_____

_____

_____

_____

_____

_____

_____

Kids

Everyone knows that parents are allowed a tax credit for their children, but did you know that special credits apply to adoption, or that as a parent you receive **child care credits?** If you incur expenses in connection with the care of your children under age 13—or if your spouse is physically or mentally unable to care for himself or herself—you may be eligible for a tax credit to offset some of these expenses.

If you earn less than $10,380 a year, or less than $27,413 if you have a child (less than $31,152 for parents of more than one child), you may qualify for the **Earned Income Tax Credit** (EITC).

Multiple Jobs

Do you work **two jobs** or did you **change jobs** during the year? You may have overpaid Social Security tax. In 2001, the Social Security tax (at 6.2 percent of your salary) is capped at $80,400 in earnings. If you have two employers, each withdrawing 6.2 percent from your paycheck, you may be overpaying. You can collect these excess payments as credits against your income tax.

Education

The **Taxpayer Relief Act of 1997** created the following significant tax credits:

When God shuts a door, he opens a window.
—JOHN RUSKIN
WRITER

- The **Hope Scholarship Tax Credit** for undergraduate study. You can claim a credit against your federal income taxes for up to $1,500 per student in your family per year. The Hope credit applies only for the first two years of post-secondary education, such as college or vocational school. It does not apply to graduate and professional-level programs.

- Have you wanted to go back to school but thought you couldn't afford it? With the **Lifetime Learning Credit** for graduate or undergraduate study, maybe you can. You can claim a credit of up to $1,000 per student in your family per year. The Lifetime Learning Credit applies to graduate-level and professional degree courses as well as undergraduate courses, including instruction to acquire or improve job skills.

Assignment

Learn about tax credits. Figure out which tax credits are available to you and your family, figure out how you can take advantage of them, and list all of this here.

Week 2: Making the Most of Your Deductibles

Deductibles fall into these general categories:

- Medical and dental expenses
- Interest payments on mortgage and certain loans
- Charitable contributions
- Casualty and theft losses
- Job expenses and other miscellaneous expenses

One of the most important techniques is to **bundle expenses** to meet the IRS's category-specific thresholds.

Assignment

Determine whether itemizing your deductibles can save you money. Give some serious thought to the deductibles described on the following pages. Visit www.irs.ustreas.gov or contact the IRS to determine the floor percentage (the minimum percentage of your taxable income) you must meet to claim deductions in each category. List possible deductions here.

_____

_____

_____

_____

_____

_____

_____

_____

_____

_____

_____

_____

_____

_____

_____

_____

_____

_____

_____

_____

_____

_____

_____

_____

_____

_____

Have You Overlooked Any Deductibles?

MEDICAL EXPENSES

To deduct your medical expenses, they need to add up to at least 7.5 percent of your adjusted gross income (AGI). That level is not commonly reached. But if you know there will be a large medical expense in your family, consider scheduling elective medical procedures (such as having wisdom teeth pulled) in the same year in order to *bundle* those expenses and meet the IRS's floor.

If your doctor recommends a service, it doesn't have to be performed by a doctor to be tax deductible. Physical therapy equipment or professional massage therapy, for example, can be bundled with your medical expenses as long as it is prescribed by your doctor. It's a good idea to get a written note from your doctor saying you need such services as proof for the IRS.

MISCELLANEOUS EXPENSES

Many miscellaneous expenses are deductible, assuming that they total at least 2 percent of your adjusted gross income when combined. Such cost categories include the following:

- Preparation materials, advice, or resources to help you file your taxes or to help you with your investments.

- Subscription fees for any professional journals and magazines that are related to your work.

- Annual dues paid to a professional society or union.

- Job hunting expenses (e.g., resumes, travel fees, and phone calls).

- Aside from your basic commute, if you use your car for business you can claim a deduction for the mileage (32.5 cents per mile), as well as for any tolls and parking fees.

- Donating unwanted items—such as clothes, furniture, or office equipment—to a charity. The wholesale value is deductible, along with 14 cents per mile if you use your car in the process.

- Consider donating stocks and bonds as charitable contributions. You will avoid capital gains taxes on them.

WORK-RELATED EXPENSES

A good thing to remember about work-related expenses, such as buying a home computer, is that the expense must cover something you legitimately use for work purposes. *But it doesn't have to be something you need*—that is, something you couldn't do your job without. Save your receipts, and get a letter from your employer stating that you do use a particular item for work if you feel uncomfortable or think it appears at all unusual.

STUDENT LOAN INTEREST

With the **Student Loan Interest Deduction,** taxpayers who have taken loans to pay the cost of attending an eligible educational institution for themselves, their spouse, or their child may deduct the interest they pay on these student loans, up to $2,500 a year.

FLEXIBLE TIMING

Writing a check for one of your deductibles a few weeks earlier (or getting married, for that matter) can affect that year's taxes. Be flexible in December!

Keep Accurate and Detailed Records!

If you are deducting car mileage, for example, keep a notebook or a dictaphone in your car. If you are deducting work-related meals and entertainment (you need to show a receipt) for expenses over $75, make sure you record the names of the people you entertain, their businesses, the subjects you discuss, and the name and location of the establishment.

Home Equity Loans

We know we warned you **against** taking out home equity loans, but if you are *certain* you can and will repay it, paying off credit card balances, car loans, and other such debts with a home equity loan will make those interest payments tax deductible.

Define the distinction between someone who is trying to swindle the government with false claims and someone who carefully, if not meticulously, takes advantage of all legal rights as far as tax savings are concerned. How can you minimize your taxes fairly?

_____

_____

_____

_____

_____

_____

_____

_____

_____

_____

_____

_____

_____

_____

_____

_____

_____

_____

Week 3: Be a Tax-Smart Investor

Here we ask you to return to your journal pages for Chapter 5. Rethink your decisions. Make sure you have considered tax issues carefully. What are the tax-related consequences of your investing decisions? Record them here. If you don't know, do some research to find out.

> Serious wealth builders must keep the tax man at bay. In other words, your investment strategy should include a tax strategy as well.
> —EARL G. GRAVES
> ENTREPRENEUR

_____

_____

_____

_____

_____

_____

_____

_____

_____

_____

_____

_____

_____

_____

_____

_____

_____

_____

_____

_____

_____

_____

_____

_____

_____

_____

_____

Remember that **municipal and government bonds pro-vide tax-exempt earnings.**

Don't forget about those **tax-deferred investment plans,** such as 401(k)s and IRAs.

Don't forget the **capital gains tax.** When you sell a stock and make a profit, you'll be taxed for it. Long-term capital gains taxes (if you've held the stock for more than one year) range from 10 to 20 percent. If you've held the stock for less than one year, the tax is significantly higher.)

You can deduct up to $3,000 in losses for capital gains tax. If you've had a bad year—only capital losses—you can deduct up to $3,000 from your income. When trying to decide whether to sell (and pay capital gains tax) or hold on (and pay tax on dividend income), think about your tax income bracket. If it's high, you might just want to pay the capital gains tax, instead of dividend payments taxed at your income rate. Try not to become too consumed by capital gains tax. Income is income, even if it is taxed. If you have the opportunity to make a lot of money on an investment, the best bet is often to take it!

The **wash sale rule** is designed to prevent people from creating artificial capital losses. The rule says you can't claim a loss from sale of a security (such as stock) if you buy the identical security as a replacement within the period beginning 30 days before the sale and ending 30 days after the sale.

Trying to decide between a **tax-exempt mutual fund** or a **taxable** one? Some people are misled by the "tax-free" appeal. Generally, tax-exempt funds make less money than taxable funds. So you have to determine your **taxable equivalent yield.**

Assignment

Pick a tax-exempt fund you would consider using, and complete the following worksheet to determine its annual rate of return.

Determining Your Taxable Equivalent Yield

1. Your marginal tax rate according to your income (see following table)

Tax Rate

Filing Status	28%	31%	36%	39.6%
Single	$27,050	$65,550	$136,750	$297,350
Married filing jointly	45,200	109,250	166,500	297,350
Married filing separately	22,600	54,625	83,250	148,675
Head of household	36,250	93,650	151,650	297,350
Qualifying widow(er)	45,200	109,250	166,500	297,350

2. Subtract line 1 from 100 _____

3. Annual rate of return for chosen tax-deferred fund _____

4. Divide line 3 by line 2 _____

This is your taxable equivalent yield. You have to earn more than this yield on a taxable bond or fund to make it a better deal.

Investing under your children's names? Each of your children can earn $700 in investment income, tax-free.

Investing in real estate? Consider the **Low-Income Housing Investment Tax Credit,** which is an incentive from the federal government to invest in low-income housing projects. The Low-Income Housing Tax Credit program is a tool for private developers and nonprofit entities to construct or rehabilitate affordable rental units.

Week 4: Getting Help

The Marriage Question

To file separately or together? Most likely you'll save by filing together, but every case differs. The solution is simple: Calculate it both ways and see which comes out cheaper.

Delayed Gratification Pays Off

Think twice about instant returns. You can be charged fees as high as 20 to 30 percent.

Learn More

None other than the IRS itself recommends the following books:

J.K. Lasser's Your Income Tax 2001, J.K. Lasser Institute (John Wiley & Sons, Inc., 2000).

The Motley Fool Investment Tax Guide 2001, Roy A. Lewis and Selena Maranjian (Motley Fool, 2001).

The Ernst & Young Tax Guide 2001, Peter W. Bernstein, editor (John Wiley & Sons, Inc., 2000).

Taxes for Dummies 2001 Edition, Eric Tyson and David J. Silverman (Hungry Minds, Inc., 2000).

J.K. Lasser's Taxes Made Easy for Your Home-Based Business, Gary W. Carter (John Wiley & Sons, Inc., 2000).

422 Tax Deductions for Businesses and Self-Employed Individuals, Bernard B. Kamoroff (Bell Springs, 2001).

Enrolled Agents

Consider hiring an enrolled agent if you need help with your taxes. Enrolled agents are former or current IRS agents who

> The best thing you can do for poor folks is not be one.
> —Isaac "Reverend Ike" Bruce Preacher

Handling Your Taxes | **133**

worked for the IRS for at least five years. They are highly specialized, trained by the federal government, and—unlike some other tax-practitioners you may encounter—their profession has been regulated by Congress since 1884! Visit www.naea.org for information and updated taxpayer tips, or call (800) 424-4339.

If You Find Yourself in Real Trouble

The Taxpayer Advocate Service can help you if you've tried unsuccessfully to resolve a problem with the IRS or have a significant hardship as a result of a tax problem. Call (877) 777-4778.

Don't pay a federal tax bill too long before it is due. It's an interest-free loan to the IRS.

Myth

Getting a big refund is a good thing for your finances. In fact, when you get a big chunk of cash as a refund, it means you're paying too much in taxes each month. You're essentially lending money to the government and earning no interest on it. Conversely, it's always difficult to come up with a lump sum of money if you wind up owing money for your taxes. (This most often happens to people who either are self-employed or have significant outside income, such as from investments.) Your goal should be to strike a balance right in the middle.

Specialized IRAs

The **Education IRA** allows taxpayers to deposit up to $500 per year into an Education IRA for a child under age 18.

You pay no taxes on the capital gains, dividends, or interest that build up in a **Roth IRA** when you withdraw the money. You must be 59½, and the withdrawal of savings and gains must not be made until at least five years after your first contribution.

A contribution to a Roth IRA is not deductible from income tax. A Roth IRA, unlike a traditional IRA, has no rule requiring minimum distributions after the taxpayer reaches age 70½.

Buying a Home

You can withdraw up to $10,000 from a traditional or Roth IRA to buy a first home. You won't be charged the 10 percent additional tax on early withdrawal if you use the money within 120 days to buy, build, or rebuild a first home for yourself or a family member.

Flexible Spending Accounts

Take advantage of flexible spending accounts (medical, child care, and transit) offered by your employer. You'll see a difference at tax time.

We realize there may have been a lot of information to digest this month, depending on your prior knowledge of tax issues. Take some time to go over what you've learned.

List at least five new tax-smart tips you vow to practice:

1. _____
2. _____
3. _____
4. _____
5. _____

_____

_____

_____

_____

Notes

_____

_____

_____

Maximizing Your Earning Potential

On April 23, 2001, the American Express Company announced the appointment of Kenneth I. Chenault, 49, as chairman and CEO, effective immediately. On that day, Chenault joined an elite few African American CEOs of Fortune 500 companies, and became the first to control a financial services global giant. The announcement came as a surprise to no one, as Chenault had assumed these responsibilities unofficially on January 1 of that year, when he took the reigns from former CEO Harvey Golub. The transition was announced long in advance by Golub, who described his close working relationship with Chenault as a "horizontal" one. Chenault now sits at the helm of this 151-year-old travel and financial services powerhouse in volatile and competitive times for the company. How he will face the challenges that lie ahead can most likely be measured by the way he has handled challenges in the past: with innovation, diligence, and integrity.

A graduate of Bowdoin College and Harvard Law School, Chenault began his career at a Wall Street law firm. At the management consultancy firm Bain & Company, he began his pattern of rapid promotion. He left Bain for American Express in 1981. Not long after joining, Chenault made a characteristic career decision. He chose a high-risk position as vice president for marketing of the merchandising-services division—a poorly organized, less successful division—over a secure line job in the heart of the business.

After devising a strategic plan to turn the failing division around, Chenault was promoted to head of the division. Under his leadership, revenues from merchandising services soared from $150 million to $500 million.

He'd made his mark and was promoted to the charge card division, where he would be promoted three more times between 1986 and 1989. As the company faced the possibility of becoming obsolete in the face of competition from Visa and MasterCard, Chenault pushed for change, even commissioning studies which concluded that the AmEx brand was losing its once superior value.

Over the next 10 years, Chenault would continue to make hard choices and implement changes that resulted in unprecedented success.

The people who have known Chenault in a variety of arenas describe him with astonishing consistency as a true leader, with a depth of belief that is inspiring to those around him. Harking back to his days at Bowdoin, where he was an active member of the college's Afro-American Club, Chenault continues to be dedicated to promoting other African Americans in business and to supporting his community.

Offering advice, Chenault says, "Dedicate yourself to a core set of values. Without them, you will never be able to find personal fulfillment and you will never be able to lead effectively."

Reflecting on Chenault's story is the perfect foundation on which to make a vow to maximize your own earning power. In so many ways, his climb to groundbreaking success contains the key elements of what it takes to get ahead in today's climate. This job market is a volatile, exciting, global, technology-driven, and unpredictable place, with the days of company loyalty long gone. You have to think of yourself as your own commodity, your own ever-evolving project, and be ready to meet the challenges of your profession. Even if you are not in business, rapid changes in the New Economy will affect you.

If you're a photographer, are you up to date on the latest in digital imaging? If you're an editor, are you prepared to weather the next media megamerger? If you aspire to work for a Fortune

500 company, are you ready for a global challenge? In order to succeed, you need to strategize to match your skills to the needs of the marketplace. Over the next four weeks, we'll explore the many angles from which you can approach your new project: *you*.

Make a commitment to short- and long-term changes in your professional life today.

Where do you stand right now in comparison to where you'd like to be? Brainstorm about how you will begin the work of strategizing. Write your ideas here.

_____

_____

_____

_____

_____

_____

_____

_____

_____

_____

_____

_____

_____

_____

_____

_____

How well do you know the **company** you work for and the **industry** in which you work? You can't expect to move ahead unless you know the cutting-edge trends in your business and can see where your employer stands. Your company's web site and other business sites, such as www.hoovers.com, can provide you with lots of salient information. Chenault was not afraid to benchmark AmEx's status against other companies. In an organization that was as old school as they come, his colleagues often preferred to turn a blind eye to the troubles and rest on the laurels of the company's past. He knew that was a mistake.

Give some serious thought to **education.** Would going back to school help you advance your career? For some, going back and finishing that bachelor's degree could mean admission to a whole new range of positions and income. For others, attaining an MBA or other graduate degree could provide the competitive edge you need to break through a plateau. But let's not limit our discussion of education to degree programs alone. Nondegree programs, such as executive education and optional employee training programs, can do wonders to advance a career. The old saying is true: Knowledge is power.

Adopt a philosophy of lifelong learning. Make sure that you read about and remain aware of the latest trends in your field. Ask questions. Take advantage of your local university or alma mater and attend lectures and conferences. Keep in touch with your alumni association and network, network, network!

Networking, creating meaningful connections and relationships that you can call on as you advance through your career, is one of the most valuable things you can do for yourself. Some people are turned off when they hear the term *networking.* They think of insincere opportunists who scramble to shake hands with whomever they deem important. This is not the kind of networking we're referring to. We are talking about creating and sustaining *meaningful* relationships.

All of your life, you learn from people, learn with people, and teach others. You collaborate on ideas and problem solving. We are simply urging you to maintain and enrich the relationships you have and be open to seeking new ones. Get involved in professional organizations. Let people know when you're looking for a job. Seek out mentors. Become a mentor to a younger colleague.

Reflect on some of the important relationships you've established at work. Are you maintaining them? Do you seek out new relationships? How do you go about it? How can you do better?

_____

_____

_____

_____

_____

_____

_____

_____

_____

_____

_____

_____

_____

_____

_____

_____

_____

_____

_____

Your personal relationships can have a huge effect on the success of your career, which brings us to our final topic: What role does your **personality** play in your success? This month, we ask you to reflect on your professional persona: Describe your leadership qualities, entrepreneurial spirit, and ability to display confidence in yourself as well as instill confidence in others.

How well do you negotiate with others? To what degree do those who work with you admire and respect you?

_____

_____

_____

_____

_____

_____

_____

_____

_____

_____

_____

_____

_____

_____

_____

_____

_____

Finally, **speak up!** Countless success stories attest to the simple fact that you won't get what you want unless you ask for it. Make it clear to your supervisors from the beginning that you plan to advance quickly and that you have very high standards for your own performance. Discuss your position and your performance with your supervisor. Take advantage of midyear and year-end reviews, but don't limit your discussion to those times. Your official review is often too late to ask for that promotion or more than the standard raise.

We've given you a lot to consider—but you've got a lifetime to employ what you learn. So let's get started.

Week 1: Devising a Strategic Plan

What's your dream job? Describe it in detail. Be creative and don't worry so much about how realistic it is. This is an opportunity for you to brainstorm about what you really want to do. Let your imagination take flight.

_____

_____

_____

_____

_____

_____

_____

_____

_____

_____

Now, let's scale back. Take the most important elements of your dream job and think about them in the context of your career. Devise a realistic, yet inspiring, career goal. For example, if you've always wanted to be a writer, think of new responsibilities you can take on at work that might involve some sort of writing.

_____

_____

_____

_____

_____

_____

_____

_____

_____

_____

_____

_____

_____

_____

_____

_____

_____

_____

_____

_____

_____

When I rejoined Morgan Stanley out of business school in 1982, I wrote down on the back of an envelope, which I still have on file in my office, a set of goals that I wanted to attain over a period of time . . . I was 26 years old when I wrote down those goals . . . I'm one year ahead of that schedule because I made partner in 7 years instead of 8. I do believe that writing it all down made a difference.
—WILLIAM M. LEWIS JR.
INVESTMENT BANKING EXECUTIVE

Assignment

You've written down your ultimate professional goal. Now, work backward from there and plan out the necessary steps. Depending on your age, set incremental goals starting at six months from now. Have a six-month goal, a 1-year goal, a 5-year goal, a 10-year goal, a 20-year goal, and so on. What problems or obstacles do you anticipate? What will you have to do in the short term to reach your long-term goals? Study people who have achieved what you wish to achieve. How did they do it? **Write everything down.** This is important. Make a commitment to yourself and to your career. Revisit and revise your strategic plan often. It will change—perhaps even dramatically—and that's fine. Just keep conscious track of it.

> Aim high and manage your own career. Don't rely on your company to do it for you.
> —IRA D. HALL
> CORPORATE EXECUTIVE

It Never Hurts to Look Around

Even if you're happy in your current job, make sure you're aware of what's out there. Develop relationships with executive recruiters to identify new career opportunities. Offer yourself as a reference to talented former colleagues and employees so that recruiters will get to know you and your work. Find out what's available by checking the papers and web sites that list job openings. Go to the web sites of your company's competitors and see what their human resources pages are posting.

Tips from the Experts

Human resources leaders in the financial industry assert that one of the top things you can do to move your career forward is to take an international position, even if just for one year. Not to mention that the experience of living abroad is invaluable, something you will look back on for the rest of your life.

Week 2: Education Success Story

from Black Enterprise, *February 2001*

Anita Womack was among the lucky ones in 1990. With a bachelor's degree in accounting, she landed a job right out of college working with the Controller's Organization, a division of AT&T Corporation that is responsible for the consolidation of financial information for external reporting. But it wasn't long before she was looking to make a change. In 1993, she decided to go back to school and get her MBA.

"At the time, I supported a lot of the technical divisions within various business units of the company," says Womack, 32. "I wanted to broaden my understanding of the technical arena. Because my background was in business, an MBA seemed to be the more logical route." In addition, courses in information systems were built into the curriculum, and many of her electives were technology related.

Prior experience and an MBA facilitated her lateral as well as vertical moves. "It helped to speed up the process," says Womack, whose starting salary was in the mid-30,000s. By the time she left AT&T in 1998, it had shot up to a little more than $52,000.

Today, Womack is an applications consultant with a German-based software company with U.S. headquarters in Newtown Square, Pennsylvania. Her role is to assess a company's business processes and configure appropriate proprietary software. Major clients include Barnesandnoble.com and Delta Airlines.

Womack has seen her pay increase 30 percent (between bonus and salary) in the last two years. Not only will pursuing continuing education boost your earning power, it will help you avoid becoming "jobsolete."

Womack loves what she does now. "The [best] thing about being a consultant is that you are not static; you are constantly learning new things." She adds that the "exposure to so many different industries and business processes increases your skills set tremendously."

> What's the difference between a good job and a great career? A strong educational foundation.
> —KEITH H. WILLIAMSON
> CORPORATE EXECUTIVE

Where do you see room for improvement in your own educational background? Would it make sense for you to go back to school? If not, where are your knowledge gaps?

_____

_____

_____

_____

_____

_____

_____

_____

_____

_____

_____

_____

_____

Assignment

- Take a step toward seeking some form of education: Look into going back to school; sign up for a class; register for a conference; create your own course by choosing a subject you need to learn about and designing a reading list.

- If you want to go back and get a degree but can't at this time, take one course, or do research on schools and scholarships so that you're ready when the opportunity presents itself.

- Vow to always make learning a part of your life.

- Are you computer literate? If not, take a starter course and become tech-savvy. Regardless of your line of work or your age, you need to know your way around a computer and the Internet.

Week 3: Personal Traits that Advance Your Career

Assignment

Leadership, Entrepreneurial Spirit, and Integrity

This week, mull these three characteristics over in your mind. Vow to incorporate, in your own way, some essence of each these qualities in the way you do your job.

Good leaders have vision. What does vision mean to you? What is your professional vision?

_____

_____

_____

_____

_____

_____

_____

_____

_____

_____

_____

_____

_____

_____

_____

If you have no confidence in self you are twice defeated in the race of life. With confidence you have won even before you have started.
—MARCUS GARVEY
   PIONEERING
   REVOLUTIONARY LEADER

Entrepreneurs take risks. They don't try to repeat what's been done before; they make up their own rules and standards. Keep an eye out for stories in the press or in the bookstore about successful entrepreneurs (try *Titans of the B.E. 100s* by Derek T. Dingle). What traits do they have in common? Entrepreneurs, by definition, are businesspeople who break out and start their own businesses, but it's been said that one can exert an entrepreneurial spirit even within a large, traditional corporation.

How can you take the lessons from stories of successful entrepreneurs and apply them to your own career?

_____

_____

_____

> No matter how much you invest in a company, if you don't have a vision and the ability to get your people to rally around it, you won't be successful.
> —LLOYD G. TROTTER
> CORPORATE CEO

_____

_____

_____

_____

_____

_____

_____

_____

_____

_____

_____

_____

Can you, as the overused expression goes, think outside the box? Think of an instance when you have been required to solve a problem by unconventional means.

> Being prepared to seize opportunities when they present themselves is the essence of success.
> —STANLEY O'NEAL
> INVESTMENT BANKING EXECUTIVE

_____

_____

_____

_____

_____

_____

_____

_____

_____

_____

_____

_____

_____

_____

_____

_____

_____

_____

What are your key personal values? Where do they come from? Do you believe that you have displayed integrity in the workplace? Think of an instance when you have not. Why? How should you have handled the situation?

_____

_____

_____

_____

_____

_____

_____

_____

_____

_____

_____

_____

_____

_____

_____

_____

_____

Week 4: Demanding What You Deserve

What percentage, honestly, do you give of yourself at work? How
can you do better?

_____

_____

_____

_____

_____

> He who loves money must
> labor.
> —AFRICAN PROVERB

_____

_____

_____

_____

_____

> The most important lesson I've learned is that you have to have the ability to give 100 percent effort and sustain it. Most people think that operating at [their] 95 percent level is giving an A effort. That's the level that most very good people operate at. But just think what a difference that extra 5 percent could make. It builds upon itself. Learn how to give everything you have to give.
> —THOMAS W. JONES
>   CORPORATE EXECUTIVE

If it's not 100 percent (if we are truthful, very few of us can answer 100), why isn't it? Do you have demands outside of work that prohibit you from giving your all? Is your job not what you really want to be doing? Would you be giving more if your work were more fulfilling?

_____

_____

_____

_____

_____

_____

_____

_____

_____

_____

_____

_____

_____

_____

_____

_____

_____

_____

Assignment

Start the ball rolling to seek a pay increase, promotion, or both by speaking to your boss, but *only if you feel your performance justifies the raise*. If you're not quite up to par, your assignment is different. Begin making a change for the better. Put in more hours. Ask to take on additional responsibility. Offer to help coworkers with their projects. After a few months of consistently improved performance, have a conversation with your supervisor and ask what he or she thinks you need to do to earn a promotion and pay raise.

Tips for Negotiating a Better Salary

- The best time to negotiate is when you start your job. It will be more difficult—but by no means impossible—to do so later.

- Arm yourself with the facts. Be able to present examples of competitive salaries in comparable positions.

- Don't forget that you are not negotiating for your paycheck alone. Keep the following forms of compensation in mind: bonuses, stock equity, savings and pension plans, holidays and vacation time, employee training, health and wellness benefits, and care plans for children or elderly relatives.

- Practice your pitch ahead of time by doing some role-playing.

- You are in a much better bargaining position if you have a competing offer. If you're unhappy with your position at work, it may be a good idea to pursue other job offers, even if you're not certain you want to leave your company. Or, have a plan, such as going back to school if you leave your job.

• You should by no means offer up the details (i.e., exact salary) of your other options.

• Don't be afraid to take the initiative in the conversation when you feel it's appropriate.

• If the job or position is new, avoid discussing salary before the offer is official.

• A very powerful negotiation strategy is to let the other person know, up front, what it would take to make you happy. This assures the other person that the negotiation won't go on indefinitely. (Of course, you need to have a clear idea yourself of what will make you happy to use this technique.)

• If a back-and-forth exchange ensues, stop pushing when you are no longer receiving positive feedback or any concessions in your favor.

• If you're offered a new job and salary, do not accept it on the spot, no matter how appealing it sounds. Be gracious and honest about your enthusiasm, but politely say that you need to go over everything one more time and will respond the next day or at another specified time.

Notes

_____

_____

_____

_____

_____

Helping to Strengthen Your Community

Congresswoman Maxine Waters is a devoted public servant and is considered by many to be the most powerful black woman in American politics. An outspoken advocate for people of color, women, children, and the poor, she has sponsored countless bills and initiatives that help disadvantaged people build financial independence and work to transform depressed neighborhoods into vibrant, enterprising communities.

Among her many projects, she helped found the Maxine Waters Employment Preparation Center in the Los Angeles unified school district, as well as a program designed to connect young people in public housing with employment opportunities. "I take great satisfaction from working with people who others don't feel are worthy of a lot of time and effort," she says. "Women in drug rehab, the children of welfare, ex–gang members. When I can see that my work is not only appreciated but changing lives, that reinforces me."

Her career in public service began as a teacher and volunteer coordinator in the Head Start program in Los Angeles. "In a way," she says, "my life began then too." Waters went on to become a tireless defendant of justice and a leader who is not afraid to speak her mind, even when her opinion is not the most popular. Her standout political career has rendered her an exemplary public figure and a passionate advocate on whom the people of Los Angeles and countless other Americans have grown to depend on.

When you hear about people giving of themselves for causes they believe in, what's your reaction? Do you admire their efforts? What are you doing to help your community? What can you do now?

_____

_____

_____

_____

_____

_____

_____

_____

_____

_____

_____

_____

Most of us have the best of intentions when it comes to making an effort to support our communities and people in need. We believe in doing it, we plan to do it, but somehow countless obstacles get in our way. Some people are so busy they never seem to get around to making contributions of either time or money. Others feel too financially strapped to donate money and too powerless to volunteer. Many of us feel overwhelmed by the vastness of the need out there and don't know quite where to begin. But as with most things for the good, simply beginning can feel so great!

Many churches practice **tithing,** the idea that everyone in the congregation contributes 10 percent of their salaries to the church. Donating at least 10 percent of your income to your community, whether through your church or in some other way, should be your goal. If you are not in a solid enough financial position at the moment, there are always other ways in which you can make a contribution. Even if you can afford only a very modest donation to the cause of your choice, *it still makes a difference.* Nonprofit groups try to make it as easy as possible for contributors to make their donations. Do some soul searching. If you volunteer or choose to contribute to a cause that means something to you personally, the chances that you will keep up your involvement over time will be greatly increased. Pick a specific need you'd like to address, or give to your church or to an organization that spreads its funds over a number of worthy causes, such as the United Way. Keep in mind that there are very likely causes right outside your door, in your community, that need your help.

If you can't afford to contribute financially, volunteer work can be one of the most worthwhile and fulfilling projects you'll take on, and you can accomplish quite a bit by contributing very modest amounts of your time. Over the next four weeks, we will ask you to evaluate your current levels of contribution and give some thought to what else you can do to help strengthen your community.

What is your level of contribution now? Are there causes you have always meant to support or organizations whose work you especially admire? How can you start to contribute to them now?

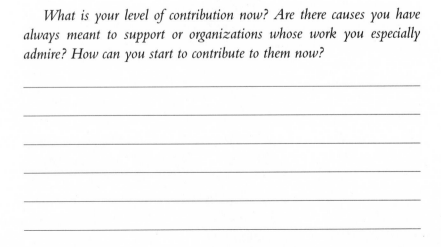

_____

_____

_____

_____

_____

_____

_____

_____

_____

What are your talents and interests? Were you into team sports as a kid? If so, consider volunteering as a coach in your community. Are you a voracious reader? Think about sharing your love of books by reading to hospitalized children or by volunteering for an adult literacy program. Was your college scholarship the key factor that eventually led to your financial success? Why not make a donation to your alma mater? The point is, everyone should seek out a way to contribute that is personally meaningful.

Once you make the vow to use a portion of your wealth to strengthen your community, it will put your wealth-building efforts in a larger, more meaningful context. Join the ranks of those who are inspired to succeed financially so that they will be in a position to give back.

Week 1: Evaluating Your Current Level of Giving

Think about the ways in which you give to your community now. What financial contributions do you consistently make, including through your church? How do you give your time to people in need in either a structured or unstructured way? How can you do better?

_____

_____

_____

_____

_____

_____

_____

_____

_____

_____

_____

_____

_____

_____

_____

_____

_____

_____

_____

_____

_____

_____

> I will not stop trying to get black people—those who can afford it—to write big checks and make meaningful contributions to worthwhile causes. Until we start doing it, we are perpetuating the notion that we're victims and that others need to take care of us.
>
> —WILLIAM M. LEWIS JR.
> INVESTMENT BANKING EXECUTIVE

Assignment

Tally up the financial donations you make. Make the closest estimate you can of your total annual giving. Is it at least 10 percent of your annual income? Could you be giving more? Take a look at your monthly budget and try to find a way to set aside even a modest amount of money for donations. Set a contribution goal for a year from now, as well as another more ambitious goal further in the future.

_____

_____

_____

_____

_____

_____

A Checklist for Givers

The sad unfolding saga of New York's Hale House clearly shows that it is not enough for an organization to have an admirable mission. To ensure that your money is not wasted, you must know it will be properly administered. Here are some things to look for when evaluating a charity or nonprofit organization. Once the group checks out, you are ready to give freely.

1. Is the exact name of the organization clear and recognizable? (Some groups have names that sound similar to those of well-known charities. Be clear about which group is which.)

2. What is the purpose of the organization (e.g., finding a cure for a disease)?

3. Is the organization a for-profit, nonprofit, or professional association?

4. How does the group achieve its goals or provide service?

5. What percentage of the group's funding comes from individuals, corporations, and foundations? The Foundation Center

(www.fdncenter.org) is a resource on grant-seeking and funding procedures.

6. How much of your dollar is used for charitable purposes? (It should be at least 60 cents.)

7. Is information made available voluntarily and in a timely manner?

8. Does the organization have a recent annual report and IRS Form 990?

9. Does the organization have 501(c)(3) legal status, which makes contributions tax deductible? Check at www.irs .ustreas.gov/prod/bus_info/eo/.

10. Is the charity or organization registered with the proper state or local government office?

From *Black Enterprise,* July 2000.

Week 2: Community Development

Affectionately known as "Miss D.C.," Anita Brown is building an educational community that branches from her Washington, D.C., home throughout the country and across continents, one modem at a time. The founder of the nonprofit organization Black Geeks Online, Brown's mission is to get African Americans online and bridge the widening gap between technology haves and have-nots. Beginning with a meeting of 18 friends in her Washington home, Black Geeks has grown to a membership of more than 25,000 adults and children.

Dubbed "the best known black woman on the Web" by *Wired* magazine, Brown has created the Taking IT to the Streets initiative, which conducts teach-ins for African American communities. On her web site, Brown describes them as "offline expos" that "have demonstrated that Net-literate volunteers make excellent trainers and role models: Kids instruct other kids, women encourage reluctant women, and black netpreneurs own the companies that donate the computers, multimedia software, dial-up service, etc."

One of Brown's main concerns is educating parents as well as children about technology and the New Economy. She sat on the Internet and Society 2000 panel at Harvard University, where she expressed her concern over computer-literacy programs that simply supply schools with equipment and leave out valuable lessons on how to use the Internet to access its true benefits. As quoted in the *Boston Globe,* Brown said, "None of this money is going to train people. They're just creating new consumers, and the last thing poor people need to do is to find a new electronic mall."

Brown is a living example of how far a little instruction can go. In 1994, her brother introduced her to the Internet, and she was very reluctant to get onboard. What sold her was the Internet's incredible ability to facilitate communication and broker information. Now she's taking that ability and putting it to use to empower the computer illiterate at home and around the world.

Assignment

Do some research. Check out local chapters of national nonprofit organizations such as the United Way, the Urban League, or the NAACP. Check with your church or local government offices to find out what kinds of community projects are underway that you might want to join.

How can you help to strengthen your public school or library system? Brainstorm about the different ways you can make a contribution right in your neighborhood and **commit to it.**

_____

_____

_____

_____

_____

_____

_____

_____

_____

_____

_____

_____

_____

_____

_____

Improving the community in which you live helps everyone, including yourself. Smart property owners know that improved schools, economic growth, and safer, cleaner streets mean higher property values.

Visit the web site for the U.S. Department of Housing and Urban Development (www.hud.com) for information on national empowerment zones.

❧

Give some thought to the place where you live. Do you see people who are in need? Do you think your community is an enriching, supportive place for children to grow up in? In today's sometimes splintered society, do you feel connected to your community?

What can you do to improve the life of your community?

_____

_____

It doesn't take much to make a great change in a community. You can do it by reading to a child. You can do it by volunteering at a soup kitchen. You can do it by visiting an older shut-in. You can do it by cleaning up a neighborhood. You can do it by mentoring, getting involved, setting an example, having a positive impact on a child's life.

—KEN CHENAULT
CORPORATE EXECUTIVE

_____

_____

_____

_____

_____

_____

_____

_____

_____

_____

_____

_____

_____

Week 3: Donating Your Time

Make It a Family Affair

Set the right example for your children by providing them with
the positive life experience of helping others. You can do many
things together—for example, serve lunch or dinner at a soup
kitchen. It will also teach your children gratitude for their own
blessings. We'll explore this area further in Chapter 10.

*What are you good at? Think about ways in which you could use
your talents to make a contribution.*

_____

_____

_____

_____

Imagine what a harmonious
world it could be if every
single person, both young
and old, shared a little of
what he is good at.
—Quincy Jones
  Musician, composer,
  and producer

_____

_____

_____

_____

_____

_____

_____

_____

_____

_____

_____

_____

_____

_____

_____

_____

_____

Visit the web site for the Independent Sector (www.independentsector.org), a coalition of leading nonprofits, foundations, and corporations strengthening not-for-profit initiatives, philanthropy, and citizen action. It suggests the following places you may not have thought of to volunteer:

- Day care centers
- Neighborhood watch groups
- Public schools, libraries, and colleges
- Halfway houses
- Community theaters

- Drug rehabilitation centers
- Fraternal organizations and civic clubs
- Retirement centers and homes for older adults
- Meals on Wheels
- Church- or community-sponsored soup kitchens or food pantries
- Museums, art galleries, and monuments
- Community choirs, bands, and orchestras
- Prisons
- Neighborhood parks
- Youth organizations, sports teams, and after-school programs
- Shelters for battered women and children
- Historical restorations, battlefields, and national parks

TIP Look for volunteer opportunities related to your professional or personal goals.

Become Politically Involved

Fight for the causes you believe in. Follow the news and send letters to your representatives. Sign petitions. Attend rallies. Consider volunteering periodically to help a political organization that you believe is doing good work, or work on the campaign of a candidate whose vision you support.

Assignment

Stop talking and start doing. *Make the time* to volunteer. If your schedule is unpredictable, there are many large volunteer organizations, such as New York Cares or Boston Cares, that publish calendars of opportunities for their volunteers so people can offer as little (one Saturday morning a month at a soup kitchen) or as much (a weekly tutoring session) as they like. Don't forget to use your church or mosque as a resource.

When Americans really began to rally against South African apartheid, how was the greatest pressure brought to bear? Economically—by freezing out those corporations that supported apartheid and benefited from it. Divestiture made all the difference.

We are in a new age of corporate citizenship and socially responsible business. As many U.S. companies move into developing nations, we need to keep an eye on the way those businesses are affecting the local people and environments, just as we remain vigilant about the impact on our own communities. Because of increased public awareness, businesses are paying closer attention to the impact of their products and practices on society. Give some thought to where you work, where you bank, where your money is invested, and what products you buy. What do you know about the ethics and values of these companies? Remember to put your money where your beliefs are. If they don't match up, *divest* and share your concerns with others.

What practices or policies would appeal to you? What would repel you?

_____

_____

_____

_____

_____

_____

_____

_____

_____

_____

The rich man who achieves a degree of greatness achieves it not because he hoards his wealth, but because he gives it away in the interest of good causes.
—BENJAMIN MAYS
SCHOLAR AND EDUCATOR

Helping to Strengthen Your Community | **169**

_____

_____

_____

_____

_____

_____

_____

_____

_____

_____

TIP Many employers will match your charitable contributions, and some will also match the time you contribute as a volunteer with monetary contributions.

Making a Difference at Work

Here are some ways you can make a difference in your professional life:

- **Become a mentor.** Keep your eye out for young—or not so young—African Americans who could use your support and guidance.

- **Do pro bono consulting.** Donate your time and professional expertise by serving as an unpaid consultant. Nonprofit organizations are businesses, too, and they can use all the help they can get. If you're a lawyer, think about offering legal advice to the disadvantaged.

- **Serve on boards of directors.** Serving on advisory boards for community or nonprofit organizations provides great professional contacts in a positive, enriching environment.

- **Support black-owned businesses.** When contracting out a job or finding a supplier, seek out a black-owned business.

- **Organize volunteer days at work.** Bond with your coworkers and have fun by cleaning up a local park or putting a fresh coat of paint on the walls of a community center. Look for a charitable organization that your company can partner with.

Success Story

from Black Enterprise, *July 2000*

Nearly 20 years ago, a group of frat brothers and graduates of Atlanta's Morehouse College pooled their money—starting with monthly contributions of $25—to create Omega Diversified Investment Consortium (basing the name on Omega Psi Phi fraternity).

In addition to investing in stocks and mutual funds, the group of 35 members bought one talk radio and two urban radio stations, the footprints of which cover Daytona Beach and Tampa, Florida, and Greenville, South Carolina. The investment club's portfolio, including investment market and venture capital projects, has a net worth valued at more than $500,000.

Omega Diversified does a lot of community outreach. For instance, there was a church that wanted to deliver meals to college students, but couldn't afford to purchase vans and other equipment. Unable to secure a traditional bank loan, the church secured a short-term loan from Omega Diversified.

"As a group we wanted to do something different," says Charles Hicks, 43, chairman of Omega's board of directors. "We approached our club like a business; we wanted to develop some products that could help empower our communities."

Looking to build wealth within the African American community, the "Ques," as they are known, established the Omega Diversified Investment Foundation, which provides scholarships to students majoring in broadcasting at historically black colleges and universities (HBCUs).

Omega Diversified is a perfect example of an organization that's doing well by doing good. Think about your own professional life.

Do you believe in socially responsible business? How can you and your employer have a more positive effect on society through the way you do business? If you're an entrepreneur, how can you use your business to do more than make money?

_____

_____

_____

_____

_____

_____

_____

_____

_____

_____

_____

_____

_____

_____

_____

_____

_____

_____

_____

_____

_____

Assignment

Think about the examples of ways you can make a contribution that you've read in this chapter and come up with a few more of your own.

_____

_____

_____

_____

_____

_____

_____

_____

Take the initiative to have a more positive impact through your professional career. We guarantee that the results of your efforts will be more meaningful than any amount of money.

Notes

_____

_____

_____

_____

_____

Teaching Your Children Well

A self-taught investor, Lynn Roney began buying stocks at the age of 27. Years later, as a longtime shareholder of McDonald's, Roney took her three-year-old granddaughter Danielle to McDonald's for her favorite food, french fries. Roney told Danielle she was glad her granddaughter liked McDonald's so much, because, as a stockholder, she was a part-owner of the restaurant. Danielle announced that she, too, wanted to become an owner, and so Roney subsequently purchased one share of McDonald's stock for her.

Roney writes in her book *Wow the Dow!,* coauthored with Pat Smith, "I purchased the stock just as a fun thing for her. She owned only 1.1984 shares, and all we had to show for it was a statement with the McDonald's logo. But it didn't matter. Danielle was so happy and proud. When we took one of her friends along to eat with us, she would say, 'Nana, tell Kandyce that I am a part owner of McDonald's!' " Over time, investing became more than just a fun story to tell. By age 14, with her grandmother's guidance Danielle had amassed a portfolio worth more than $18,000.

Wow the Dow! is a guide that teaches parents how to start investing in the stock market with their children and encourages kids to think intelligently about money. Roney and coauthor Smith also cofounded Stock MarKids, a nationally affiliated parent–child investment club. Smith's daughter Shannon is also a kid investor. Both girls are members of MarKids; each child contributes about

$20 per month toward stock purchases. It's a very democratic process—money is pooled, and the kids vote on stock choices.

Danielle and Shannon are both advocates of a **buy-and-hold** philosophy. In an article on the *Consumer Reports* web site, Danielle says about the prices of stocks fluctuating, "If they weren't good stocks, we wouldn't have gotten them in the first place." She admits that she tries not to check the price of her stocks too often in a down market so she won't "go crazy."

"Ownership bestows more than pride," Roney and Smith assert in *Wow the Dow!* "It gives people a reason to care, a reason to take on responsibility." Roney has not only given her granddaughter and the other MarKids members responsibility and countless valuable financial lessons, she's provided Danielle with a financial head start most parents could only dream of.

In this chapter, we encourage you to follow Lynn Roney's example: Take what you have recently learned (or rediscovered) about personal finance and educate others, especially young people. Have there been many instances in this past year when you've said to yourself, "If only I were younger. If only I had it to do all over again, knowing what I know now. . . ." Well, there is a young person in your life—your child, niece, nephew, neighbor, grandchild, godchild—for whom it isn't too late.

How do kids learn about work ethics or the way to relate to other people in their lives? They may learn some of this at school or from religious teaching, but generally, they learn these things at home from their parents and from the adults they are closest to. It's essentially our primary job to teach our children values. Have you ever heard yourself or a friend say, "I don't want my children to have to worry about money growing up, the way I did." That's an admirable and wonderful goal, but let's make sure that not worrying doesn't equal ignorance about finances. Find a way to strike the right balance.

Alarmingly, most schools don't teach children about finances and the responsibilities of handling money. The Jump$tart Coalition for Personal Financial Literacy, a nonprofit organization, determined in its studies that the average student who graduates from high school lacks basic skills in the management of personal financial affairs. The organization found that many are unable to balance a checkbook, and most have no insight into the basic survival principles involved with earning, spending, saving, and investing. No wonder so many young people fail at managing their first consumer credit experience and tend to establish bad financial management habits overall.

Teaching young people about credit cards is crucial. As covered in Chapter 3, on credit and debt, credit card companies have been targeting college students aggressively. You may be surprised to learn that the *Washington Post* reported in an April 2001 article that "now the industry is aiming even younger—at teenagers in high school or even middle school." This can have serious consequences if children aren't educated properly and taught the truth about credit card debt. The same article cited a study by Harvard Law professor Elizabeth Warren, which found that 120,000 people under the age of 25 filed for bankruptcy in 2000, an increase of 50 percent since 1991. You must ensure that the young people in your life won't become part of that statistic.

Some parents are finding safety and convenience in providing their children with **debit cards,** which have strict limits on available funds. This practice does have its benefits, but children need to first understand the basic value of a dollar, both earned and spent. So start there, and start early.

What was your personal experience and education regarding finances like? Did your parents and mentors actually teach you, or did you just pick things up along the way?

_____

_____

_____

_____

_____

_____

_____

_____

_____

_____

_____

_____

_____

_____

_____

_____

_____

Teaching kids about finances can be fun for both you and them. One of the best ways to do this is to get kids to invest. Start by teaching children to become financially ambitious. Share stories of successful African Americans with them. Visit www.blackenterprise.com and learn more about the Kidpreneurs program.

Finally, encourage children to pursue **careers,** not just jobs. Don't instruct kids to choose their careers solely based on how much money they'll make. Instead, teach them that once they've found a profession that they love, they should work for and demand the highest pay available in their chosen line of work. Help young people to set ambitious goals. You can do this in part by sharing your own goals with them.

This is an extremely important chapter. If we are going to improve the financial lives of African Americans, we must be committed to bringing up the next generation to be better off than we were—not merely in terms of what they earn, but in what they do with it. Make the commitment to your own children, or choose a young person you care about to mentor. Resist being an example of the old saying, "Do as I say, not as I do." Lead and _teach_ by example.

Week 1: Teach About the Realities of Money

Think long and hard about what kind of a financial role model you are for the young people in your life. What does your lifestyle say to them? What can you do to improve?

_____

_____

_____

_____

_____

_____

_____

_____

_____

_____

_____

_____

_____

_____

_____

_____

> Children have never been very good at listening to their elders, but they have never failed to imitate them.
> —JAMES BALDWIN
>   AUTHOR

Have your kids visit www.jumpstartcoalition.org to take the Reality Check quiz. Kids answer specific questions about how they plan to live and then find out how much one has to earn to reach such a standard of living.

Assignment

Teaching kids about the value of a dollar can be done in a variety of ways. Very young children start by learning the actual value of coins and bills, then move on to how much money it costs to buy what they love—toys, candy, ice cream, and the like. Depending on the age group you're targeting, you may want to pay a child for doing chores, or give him or her a sense of the range of salaries that exist for different professions and types of work. List at least five ways you'll teach the children in your life about what money represents and how it can be used.

1. _____
2. _____
3. _____
4. _____
5. _____
   _____
   _____

> My kids don't have the attitude that they deserve money, which is good. In the environment that they're being brought up in now, they are exposed to an economically diverse group of kids and that gives them a glimpse of reality. Plus, when I give them money, they know they have a limited amount and I tell them to use it wisely.
> —Vanessa L. Williams
> Actress and singer

Shopping with Your Kids

Here are a few thoughts on shopping with your kids:

- If children want special items, help them set financial goals of earning and saving to buy the items.

- Teach children the basics of comparison shopping: quality versus overpriced items and inexpensive versus cheap items.

- Explain to your children how much something expensive costs in terms of how many hours one would have to work to pay for it.

- Explain to your children the concept and rationale behind supporting black-owned businesses. Remember to teach them by your example.

- When your children are drawn to certain brands, ask them why. Discuss the power of advertising. Teach kids to read between the lines and not trust everything they hear or see on television about products.

- Help your children to be conscious spenders by encouraging them to understand the distinction between what they truly need and merely want.

Week 2: Teach About Saving, Budgeting, Credit, and Debt

Assignment

Share the Declaration of Financial Empowerment with your children. You might even fashion a junior version and have your children sign it. Explain what it really means to make such a commitment. Encourage them to make that commitment, and explain its long-term benefits. Here are some concrete steps you can take to lead your children toward making the declaration:

- Every child should open and contribute to a savings account as well as keep a piggy bank for short-term, readily available savings.

- If a child can add, subtract, and multiply, he or she can understand the basics of your household budget. Explain the day-to-day realities of cash flow, in and out.

- Make sure your children understand what a mortgage is, how credit cards work, and how loans, such as student loans and car loans, work.

- Teach kids about taxes. Show your children your paycheck. Calculate with them how much is taken out for taxes and why.

- Explain the concept of net worth. As young people they may not have a lot of assets, but on the flip side they also don't have debt!

- Choose appropriate times to have your children join you when you go over the finances.

• Teach your children to spend their money wisely—for example, for trading cards, collectible dolls, or comics that may appreciate in value.

What are the most important lessons you've learned on your wealth-building journey? Now try to boil those concepts down to plain talk at a level children will understand.

We have a powerful potential in our youth, and we must have the courage to change old ideas and practices so that we may direct their power toward good ends.
—MARY MACLEOD BETHUNE
EDUCATOR AND ORATOR

_____

_____

_____

_____

_____

_____

_____

_____

_____

_____

_____

_____

_____

_____

_____

_____

_____

_____

Web Sites for Financial Education Games

- **Escape from Knab** at www.escapefromknab.com
- **Gazillionaire** at www.lavamind.com
- **Fleet Kids** at www.fleetkid.com

Week 3: Get Kids to Invest!

When did you start investing? At what age do you wish you would have started investing? Has your attitude toward the concept of investing changed over the course of this journal? What have you learned that you'd most like to share with a young person?

_____

_____

_____

_____

_____

_____

_____

_____

_____

_____

_____

_____

_____

_____

_____

TIP Play Monopoly! It's a fun way to introduce kids to dollar values and the concept of investing.

Visit www.kidstock.com for fun and informative kid-oriented investing talk.

Assignment

Give a young person an investment as a gift, and choose the stock or fund together. There are a few mutual funds that focus on kids, such as the Steinroe Young Investors Fund, which also publishes a newsletter for kid investors. Or, help create an investment club for your kids. Get them started today!

The **Uniform Gift to Minors Act** allows you to set up a custodial account at any number of banks and mutual fund companies. Shares or funds are held in trust for at least 10 years. You can open an account with as little as $500.

Success Story

from Black Enterprise, *October 1999*

Like most of his peers, 13-year-old Amadi spends his allowance and cash gifts on PlayStation video games and sports apparel. The young athlete plays power forward on his junior high school's basketball team. But he also diligently sets aside at least 25 percent of his $15 allowance every two weeks to invest in the stock market.

Amadi, who's following in the footsteps of his mother, Janice, cofounder of Mainstream Investment Club, says he wants to learn as much as he can about investing so that he can build a solid financial foundation for the long term. That could mean saving money to help buy a car down the road or help his parents send him to college.

"I like investing and buying different stocks, because it's a good way to [accumulate wealth] and to put money back into your own pockets when you purchase shares in companies whose products you buy all the time," says Amadi. Members of the Young Investors Club take what they do very seriously. Dues are $7 a month, and anyone who fails to come up with his or her share of the pot gets hit with a $2 late fee.

Each month the members meet and report on their stock of choice. Amadi was eyeing Wendy's International (NYSE: WEN), Sara Lee (NYSE: SLE) and Coca-Cola. After examining the stocks' fundamentals—their price and earnings histories—he settled on Coke, but not for the club's portfolio. Instead, he decided to purchase shares in the soft drink maker through his parents' broker for his personal portfolio.

"I have been following Coke for a while," he explains. "We buy a lot of Coke for the house. The company also puts out a lot of other products that we buy. So I felt it was a good stock to buy."

Amadi and his fellow club members are putting into practice many of the principles outlined in past issues of *Black Enterprise for Teens* and *Kidpreneurs News,* sister publications of *BE.* These include tips on how to invest, start your own investment club, and how to manage your finances.

Visit www.better-investing.org—your kids can join the National Association of Investors Corporation. Get a free copy of *Investing in Your Future,* NAIC's student-friendly textbook for high school–aged investors.

Week 4: Inspire Ambition

We don't just want our children to be financially successful. We want them to live happy, fulfilling lives. Teach them the difference between a job and a career, between a goal and a dream, between ambition and a personal mission.

What is your definition of true ambition? How ambitious are you? How can you help your children understand ambition?

Children: I don't know what the future may hold, but I know who holds the future.
—RALPH ABERNATHY
CLERGY MEMBER AND
CIVIL RIGHTS LEADER

_____

_____

_____

_____

_____

_____

_____

_____

_____

_____

_____

_____

_____

_____

_____

_____

_____

_____

_____

_____

_____

What have you learned about the relationship between personal fulfillment and giving to others or supporting your community? Think about how you would like to share that with your children.

_____

_____

_____

Assignment

One of the primary determinants of success is education. Take an active role in your child's education. Set academic goals together. Talk about college and the application process *early;* begin when they start high school.

Did you know that thousands of dollars of fellowship and grant money for education go unclaimed each year? For more information visit the Foundation Center at fdncenter.org.

Share the principles you've learned about **maximizing your earning potential** with your kids.

It's Never Too Soon for a Credit Check

If your child or the young person you are mentoring is old enough to have paid any bills or attained a credit card, have him or her request a credit report, and analyze it together. No matter what age they are, make sure children understand the long-term consequences of not paying their bills on time.

Now, we're certainly not suggesting you send kids off to work at the age of six, but it is valuable for children to understand how hard other people have had to work in their lives to accomplish their dreams.

> I never had a chance to play with dolls like other kids. I started working when I was six years old.
> —BILLIE HOLIDAY
> JAZZ SINGER

The Power of Role Models

Teach your children about prominent African Americans. Read real-life success stories together. Try visiting www.teachervision.com for an encyclopedia of prominent African Americans.

Notes

Passing on Wealth to Future Generations

It's almost impossible to imagine a more inspirational and exemplary story than that of Oseola McCarty. When she died at age 91, McCarty had accumulated a life savings of $150,000 on a modest income from taking in washing and ironing at the small wooden-frame house in Hattiesburg, Mississippi, where she'd spent most of her life. Informed of her terminal illness two years before her death, McCarty quietly told the University of Southern Mississippi that she wanted to donate her entire savings to provide scholarships for underprivileged students. She is quoted in an article in the *New York Times* as explaining, simply, "I'm giving it away so that the children won't have to work so hard, like I did."

As a child, McCarty says, she wanted to become a nurse, but she had to drop out of school to care for sick relatives. McCarty's selfless act inspired a successful matching fundraising campaign that raised more than $300,000 for scholarships in her name. It has also inspired countless others to believe that having a modest income does not have to translate into modest impact.

Thanks to Oseola McCarty, already nine students have been provided with college scholarships. Her story is a real-life example of how wealth building with even the most humble beginnings can provide for future generations. McCarty had no children or living relative to pass her savings on to, yet she found a meaningful way to create a lasting legacy.

What McCarty lacked in education and income she more than made up for in discipline, determination, and vision. She knew what too many of us—especially in our community—fail to accept: You can't take it with you. And without proper advance planning, much of what you've worked for and amassed in your lifetime can end up being lost, squandered or redistributed in ways you would never have dreamed of or wanted. This month, we will address the subject of ensuring that the wealth you've worked so hard to build gets passed on to the next generation.

The practical topics we'll cover in this chapter—preparing a will, minimizing taxes on your estate, setting up trusts, and making charitable donations—are subjects most of us don't like to think about for many reasons. For starters, we don't want to think about being separated from our family members and loved ones. But it's precisely your concern for them that should inspire you to make sure they will be adequately provided for. You also want to make sure that your hard-earned wealth does not get swallowed up by unnecessary taxes and that the transfer of your estate will take place as smoothly as possible. Unlike in other chapters, where we have encouraged you to learn about a subject yourself and not depend on professional advisors, here we strongly encourage you to consult a lawyer when drawing up your will.

Many people mistakenly believe that wills and trusts are only for the very wealthy. This is false. If you have any assets at all, you should have a will. Otherwise, a court-appointed stranger will be in charge of allocating what you've left behind.

You'll need to choose an executor or personal representative to oversee the will. After your death, the executor will have to take inventory of your assets, protect them against loss, pursue outstanding claims, pay bills, and file and pay taxes. This is obviously quite a responsibility, and you should make the decision carefully. A spouse, a sibling, or an adult child is often a first choice, but you should factor in the emotional condition your family members will be in. Sometimes a trusted friend or lawyer is a good choice. You can also appoint coexecutors: a family member and a trusted professional, for example. Try to avoid appointing a firm or a bank, because you can't ensure that the people you currently work with at an establishment will be there at the time of your death. (With a professional executor, there will also be fees involved. You may want to account for those in the will.)

Whomever you choose, you should make sure you've gone over your will carefully with your executor and be certain this person is prepared and willing to carry out the responsibilities involved. If you have children, another very important task will be to make sure you have appointed legal guardians for them. You should give careful thought to the financial aspects of this as well. Make sure you provide for the guardians so that the children don't cause them financial hardship. If you have a child with special needs, such as a medical condition, again, make sure you have planned ahead financially.

You may also include a letter of instruction. This can address nonfinancial issues, such as your wishes for your children's religious upbringing, and can also allocate items that have more sentimental importance than material worth. Finally, this month you will reassess your life insurance policy and consider the benefits of setting up trusts to avoid tax penalties.

The larger theme we will ask you to consider over the next four weeks is this: For better or for worse, in our society, wealth is often a measure of power. The *Black Enterprise* Wealth-Building Initiative is a call to African Americans to build, maintain, and transfer wealth as a community, as a way of ensuring that each generation begins life with more power than those before it.

This may seem a daunting task, but like the cumulative effect of building personal wealth dollar by dollar, a wealthier, more powerful African American community is born one person at a time. In 1962, John F. Kennedy talked to an audience at the University of California, Berkeley, about providing for future generations: "I am reminded of the story of the great French Marshal Lyautey, who once asked his gardener to plant a tree. The gardener objected that the tree was slow-growing and would not reach maturity for a hundred years. The marshal replied, 'In that case, plant it this afternoon.'"

This journal is designed to motivate you to begin right away, and not lose track of long-term goals that may not come to fruition even in your lifetime. Try to see the future trajectory of your wealth-building journey.

What do you hope to pass on to the next generation? What legacy will you leave?

_____

_____

_____

_____

_____

_____

_____

_____

_____

_____

_____

_____

_____

_____

_____

_____

_____

_____

_____

_____

Week 1: Getting Started

What does this statement by Frederick Douglass mean to you? What do you think it means in the context of the Black Wealth-Building Initiative?

_____

_____

_____

_____

_____

_____

_____

_____

_____

> When we are noted for enterprise, industry, and success, we shall no longer have any trouble in the matter of civil and political rights.
> —FREDERICK DOUGLASS
>   ABOLITIONIST

Assignment

Get your paperwork together to begin preparing your will. Generally, you will need tax returns, bank statements, insurance policies, and a summary of your assets. There are estate planning software programs that will get your paperwork in great shape to take to a lawyer. Don't try to go it totally on your own. Tax and estate laws can be complex and are ever changing. The more organizational work you do, the less expensive your legal fees will be.

Things to Think About When Preparing a Will

- **Basic information.** The basic information you will need to provide to your lawyers includes a list of your assets and liabilities, where you want your assets to go, a choice of executor (and a successor executor), and a choice of guardian for your children (along with a successor guardian).

- **Insurance policies.** Don't leave important policy papers in your bank safe-deposit box. This will significantly slow down the process of distributing the benefits.

- **Witnesses.** Never have a beneficiary act as a witness when you sign your will.

- **Periodic review.** Make sure you review your will upon such events in your life as marriage or divorce, the birth or adoption of a child, a financial windfall, or a move to another state.

Week 2: Selecting Your Trusted Executor

Give some serious thought to the individuals you are considering as your executors or coexecutors. Even if you think you are certain, make second and third choices. If you're having trouble deciding, write out your emotional and rational reasons for each selection, along with the pros and cons of each choice.

_____

_____

_____

_____

_____

_____

_____

_____

_____

_____

_____

_____

_____

_____

_____

_____

_____

_____

_____

_____

_____

Choosing a guardian for your children in the event of your death can be one of the most difficult decisions you'll ever make. Follow the same procedure as described before. Also, be sure to ask those you choose if they are willing to assume these responsibilities. Encourage their complete candor. Only with it can you know you've made the right decision.

_____

_____

_____

_____

_____

_____

_____

_____

_____

_____

_____

_____

_____

_____

_____

_____

_____

_____

_____

Assignment

Make a final decision about an executor or guardian. If the decision is taking more than a week, set yourself a deadline. Then stick to it. Once you ask the person and they agree, set up a time to go over the details of your plans and wishes.

I wasn't really raised to consider wealth. My parents lived paycheck to paycheck. I think a lot of black parents did. Now, having gotten to a point where I don't have to worry about money, I believe that wealth is something more black families should think about. But it has to be in a realistic way. And it has to be as part of building something to pass on to children and grandchildren.
—DEBRA L. LEE
CORPORATE EXECUTIVE

Week 3: Reducing Estate Taxes

What did money and wealth mean in your family growing up? How would you like your children and grandchildren to feel about wealth?

_____

_____

_____

_____

_____

_____

_____

_____

_____

_____

_____

_____

_____

_____

_____

_____

_____

Assignment

Determine the worth of your estate. If it's less than $675,000 in total, you can have a lawyer prepare a simple will and have it notarized. If your estate totals more than $675,000, you will need to consider the impact of estate taxes. If you are married, begin the process of making sure that your assets are evenly divided to minimize taxes. As a married couple, you can shelter up to $1.35 million from estate tax for your children. Depending on the size of your estate, you may have to consider the issues related to trusts and gifting (see next section).

Other Ways to Minimize Estate Taxes

- If your assets are large enough, consider making a significant gift to a charity to reduce the taxable amount of your estate.

If you do this during your lifetime, you can also benefit from the income tax deductions.

- Use your annual gifting allowance. You can give away as much as $10,000 per year to as many individuals as you wish while you're still alive ($20,000 if you and your spouse each give a gift), tax-exempt for the recipient.

- You can provide funds for a child's higher education with a Section 529 college savings plan.

- An irrevocable trust (like the one Oseola McCarty created) can offer relief from taxes because you technically no longer have control over the assets. A revocable trust or a living trust, of course, can be called back and is included in your estate for tax purposes.

TIP Register your mutual funds and brokerage accounts as *transfer-on-death* accounts.

Week 4: Help from the Experts

Assignment

By now you should be ready to make an appointment with a lawyer and, if your estate is complex enough, a financial planner.

If you think of yourself as a bit young to think about where your wealth will be transferred, try to imagine how your priorities and point of view on wealth may change as you age.

What do you hope to learn as you mature?

If you are older and find yourself thinking about the transfer of your estate, think back on your perspective 10, 20, or even 30 years ago. *How have your priorities changed? What's the greatest change among them?*

> The man who views the world at 50 the same as he did at 20 has wasted 30 years of his life.
> —MOHAMMED ALI
>   WORLD CHAMPION BOXER

from Black Enterprise, *October 2000*

Frances Lewis sees herself as a survivor. She grew up in a poor, close-knit family in Detroit, and married when she was 21. "During our first year of marriage, my husband and I only had $27 between us," recalls Lewis, an "emancipated housewife" who went back to school in her late twenties. Her five sons were ages five, six, seven, eight, and nine when she received her bachelor's degree in elementary education from Wayne State University.

Today, the 64-year-old grandmother and soon-to-be retired educator is crafting an estate plan in order to make sure her loved ones are taken care of in the event of her death. Lewis' impressive estate comprises life insurance policies, retirement funds, several rental properties, and a Coverall cleaning franchise—Williams Lewis Connections Inc.

Lewis started saving shortly after entering the workforce in the early 1970s. As soon as she was eligible, she began participating in a 403(b) retirement savings plan (designed for civil service employees). She started with just $10 out of every paycheck.

"I still remember the exact [amount] I was making—$7,716 a year," she jokes. She gradually increased her contributions so that by the time she retires in February 2001, she will be saving over 30 percent of her biweekly salary. Over the years, Lewis also invested roughly $100,000 in real estate, then built, purchased, and later rented out property that once belonged to family members (and were willed to other relatives).

Lewis says that she and her late husband, Thomas Sr., a retired janitor with Chrysler Corporation, had wills. However, it wasn't until five years ago, after her husband's death, that she began to work seriously with a financial advisor.

She set up a custodial account for two of her grandchildren, Monique, 13, and Thomas Jr., 10, to help provide for their college education and other living expenses. She also has created and transferred the bulk of her assets into a living revocable trust, which she is transferring to First of Michigan, a division of Fahnestock.

Think about McCarty's gift to future generations and to all of us as a role model and inspiration.

If and when you can afford it, what kind of gift would you like to leave? What would make you feel proud?

_____

_____

_____

_____

_____

_____

_____

_____

_____

Notes

_____

_____

_____

_____

_____

_____

_____

_____

There's a lot of talk about self esteem these days. It seems pretty basic to me. If you want to feel proud of yourself, you've got to do things you can be proud of. Feelings follow actions.
—OSEOLA McCARTY
WASHERWOMAN AND
PHILANTHROPIST

Your Annual Review

This is it! You are nearing the end of a journey of commitment to building a better financial present and future for yourself, your family, and, by extension, all of us. Instead of presenting this chapter as an ending, we'd like you to think of it as a beginning: the beginning of your new financial life. In this chapter you'll conduct a thorough review of this past year with an eye toward continuing to move forward.

You may not have accomplished everything you hoped you would, but you've developed a solid foundation and a framework from which you can continue to build wealth. We hope that one of the most important lessons you've learned is that you *are* capable of taking your financial life into your own hands. By acting on your declaration dollar by dollar, day by day, you should be starting to see the cumulative effect of your efforts. Just like the power of compounding in investing, consistency over time has remarkable payoffs, which you are only just beginning to see.

Over the past 11 months, we've shared other people's success stories with you to illustrate key points and to inspire you to learn from their examples. Now it's your turn. Tell your own story.

What's happened to you over the past year? How has your ability to build wealth improved, and what are your plans for your financial future?

This journey has been about developing positive financial habits, the last of which is giving yourself an annual review. This month you'll write your own guidelines for a financial review that you'll keep and use for many years to come. Make it a family exercise. This will teach your children about the importance of conducting periodic self-analysis, financial and otherwise. You have to be a fair judge of yourself and push to do better in the future.

Really take your time and reflect. Go back and read through your journal entries.

Have you seen any changes in your attitude about your finances since the beginning of this year?

_____

_____

_____

_____

_____

_____

_____

_____

_____

_____

_____

_____

_____

_____

_____

_____

Week 1: Looking Back

What questions have you answered for yourself this year? What questions have you yet to answer?

_____

_____

_____

_____

_____

_____

_____

_____

> There are years that ask questions and years that answer.
> —ZORA NEALE HURSTON
> PIONEERING AUTHOR

Assignment

- **Order your credit report again.**
- Just as you did at the six-month mark, **go back through the previous five chapters and do or redo incomplete assignments.**

Week 2: Rethinking the Basics

In order to grow, we need to be constantly challenging ourselves. Outline new challenges to meet in the next year.

_____

_____

_____

_____

_____ | There is never time in the
| future in which we will
_____ | work out our salvation. The
| challenge is in the moment;
_____ | the time is always now.
| —James Baldwin
_____ | Novelist

_____

_____

_____

_____

_____

_____

_____

_____

_____

_____

Assignment

- **Complete the retirement worksheet again.** How are
  your savings? Can you up your monthly contribution?

_____

_____

_____

_____

_____

_____

_____

_____

_____

_____

_____

_____

_____

- **Go over your monthly budgets.** Determine patterns. What are your spending weaknesses?

_____

_____

_____

_____

_____

_____

_____

_____

_____

_____

_____

_____

_____

_____

- **Evaluate your investments.** How have your investments grown? Calculate how much you have paid in taxes and fees over the year. Is this too much? Should you rethink your investment strategy? Are you ready to move more money over more aggressive, high-risk investments?

> Standing ground for a race, as for an individual, must be laid on intelligence, industry, thrift and property.
> —BOOKER T. WASHINGTON
> EDUCATOR AND ORATOR

_____

_____

_____

_____

_____

_____

_____

_____

_____

_____

_____

Do business with black-owned banks and financial service companies, buy stock in well-run black-owned companies. Develop an all-around philosophy of thinking black while staying in the black.
—EARL G. GRAVES
  ENTREPRENEUR

Are you supporting your community and putting your consumer dollars toward African American owned companies? How does it make you feel? How can you do better?

_____
_____
_____
_____
_____
_____

- **Do a career assessment.** How are you progressing on your strategic plan? Edit your strategic plan.
- **How close are you to your financial goal?** Is it time to rethink your goal? Shape and refine your goal.

_____
_____
_____
_____
_____
_____
_____
_____
_____
_____
_____

_____

_____

_____

_____

_____

_____

_____

_____

_____

_____

What sacrifices have people in your life made for you? What values do you wish to instill in the young people who are close to you?

"Those who fail to plan, plan to fail." The old saying is true.
—EARL G. GRAVES
    ENTREPRENEUR

_____

_____

_____

_____

_____

_____

_____

_____

_____

_____

_____

_____

Assignment

Just as any corporation measures and reports on its financial performance, you should always conduct an annual review of your personal financial situation, in addition to your weekly or monthly review sessions. Create a worksheet of annual review guidelines that you will use every year.

Finally, **determine your net worth again.** Have you reached your goal for the end of the year? What's your goal for next year? Write about it.

My parents left everything behind in Jamaica so my two sisters and I could have a better shot at having a college education. Recognizing what they had sacrificed, I knew then that I had to be successful.
—LANCE DRUMMOND
    CORPORATE EXECUTIVE

_____

_____

_____

_____

_____

_____

_____

_____

_____

_____

_____

_____

_____

_____

_____

_____

Though you may have filled the pages of this book, we hope that you will continue to keep a financial journal. It's important to keep checks and balances on your finances, and a written record is an extremely useful tool. Also, keep yourself inspired. When you read something that motivates you, write it down in your journal. Record useful tips and facts that you come across. Continue to read financial newspapers, newsletters, and magazines; check out new and dependable web sites; and constantly build on the knowledge you've already gained. **Good luck!**

> We need to think of our personal finances as a business and approach them with the same focus and deliberation we devote to our businesses and careers.
> —Earl G. Graves
> Entrepreneur

Notes

_____

_____

_____

_____

_____

_____

_____

_____

_____

_____

_____

_____

_____

_____

_____

_____

_____

Resources

Chapter 1

"Golden Wave for U.S.," Sydney 2000: Summer Olympics Special Section, Karen Rosen. *Atlanta Constitution,* September 19, 2000

Merriam Webster's Collegiate Dictionary, Tenth Edition (Merriam-Webster, 1994).

Smart Guide to Managing Your Time, Lisa Rogak, (John Wiley & Sons, Inc., 1999).

Why Should White Guys Have All the Fun? How Reginald Lewis Created a Billion-Dollar Business Empire, Reginald F. Lewis and Blair S. Walker (John Wiley & Sons, Inc., 1995).

Psychology, Henry Gleitman (W.W. Norton, 1981).

Chapter 2

Certified Financial Planners Board of Standards, www.cfp-board.org.

"How to Invest in Uncertain Times," Andrew Tobias, *Parade Magazine,* February 18, 2001.

MSN MoneyCentral, www.moneycentral.msn.com.

"Saving Fitness: A Guide to Your Money and Financial Future" (U.S. Department of Labor, 2001)

Take a Lesson: Today's Black Achievers on How They Made It and What They Learned Along the Way, Caroline V. Clarke (John Wiley & Sons, Inc., 2001).

U.S. Department of Labor, www.dol.gov.

U.S. Social Security Administration, www.ssa.gov.

Why Should White Guys Have All the Fun? How Reginald Lewis Created a Billion-Dollar Business Empire, Reginald F. Lewis and Blair S. Walker (John Wiley & Sons, Inc., 1995).

Chapter 3

"Knowing and Understanding Your Credit" (Fannie Mae Foundation, 2000).

Managing Credit: What You Need to Know to Boost Your Buying Power, Robert McKinkey and Marc Robinson (Dorling Kindersley, 2000).

Chapter 4

Better Business Bureau, www.bbb.org.

Consumer Information Center, www.pueblo.gsa.gov.

"The NAACP Consumer Choice Guides and Report Cards," www.naacp.org.

National Consumer League, www.nclnet.org.

On Her Own Ground: The Life and Times of Madam C. J. Walker, A'Lelia Bundles (Scribner, 2001).

Chapter 5

Black Enterprise Guide to Investing, James A. Anderson (John Wiley & Sons, Inc., 2001).

The Fast Forward MBA in Investing, John Waggoner (John Wiley & Sons, Inc., 1998).

The Intelligent Investor: A Book of Practical Counsel, Fourth Edition, Benjamin Graham (HarperCollins, 1985).

"An Investment Primer," Vanguard Group, www.Majestic.vanguard.com.

Strategic Research Institute, www.srinstitute.com.

The Millionaire's Club: How to Start and Run Your Own Investment Club, Caroline M. Brown (John Wiley & Sons, Inc., 2000).

The Motley Fool Investment Guide, David Gardner and Tom Gardner (Simon & Schuster, 1996).

Take a Lesson: Today's Black Achievers on How They Made It and What They Learned Along the Way, Caroline V. Clarke (John Wiley & Sons, Inc., 2001).

Chapter 6

"Day and Night in NYC," *Harvard Law Bulletin,* Fall 1999.

Take a Lesson: Today's Black Achievers on How They Made It and What They Learned Along the Way, Caroline V. Clarke (John Wiley & Sons, Inc., 2001).

Chapter 7

The Complete Idiot's Guide to Doing Your Taxes with Turbo Tax Deluxe, Joe Kraynak (Macmillan, 1999).

Fatherhood, Bill Cosby (Doubleday/Dolphin, 1988).

U.S. Internal Revenue Service, www.irs.gov.

The Wall Street Journal Guide to Understanding Your Taxes, Scott R. Schmedel, Kenneth M. Morris, Alan M. Siegel, and Virginia B. Morris (Fireside, 1995).

Chapter 8

Against All Odds: The Entrepreneurs Who Followed Their Hearts and Found Success, Wendy Harris (John Wiley & Sons, Inc., 2000).

"Ken Chenault: The Rise of a Star," *Business Week,* December 21, 1998.

The Mind and the Heart of the Negotiator, Second Edition, Leigh L. Thompson (Prentice Hall, 2000).

Take a Lesson: Today's Black Achievers on How They Made It and What They Learned Along the Way, Caroline V. Clarke (John Wiley & Sons, Inc., 2001).

Titans of the B.E. 100s, Derek T. Dingle.

Working Without a Net: How to Survive and Thrive in Today's High-Risk Business World, Morris R. Shechtman (Prentice Hall, 1994).

Chapter 9

"Biography of Congresswoman Waters," U.S. House of Representatives Official Web Site, www.house.gov.

The Independent Sector, www.independentsector.org.

Take a Lesson: Today's Black Achievers on How They Made It and What They Learned Along the Way, Caroline V. Clarke (John Wiley & Sons, Inc., 2001).

U.S. Department of Housing and Urban Development, www.hud.gov.

Chapter 10

Black Geeks Online, www.blackgeeks.org.

Kids, Parents, and Money: Teaching Personal Finance from Piggy Bank to Prom, Willard Stawski, II (John Wiley & Sons, Inc., 2000).

"This Connector Spots Internet Gaps and Bridges Them," Patti Hartigan, *Boston Globe,* June 23, 2000.

Wow the Dow!, Lynn Roney and Pat Smith

Chapter 11

The Complete Estate Planning Guide: Updated to Include Tax Changes to 1998, Kathleen Adams and Robert Brosterman (Mentor Books, 1998).

The Complete Idiot's Guide to Wills and Estates, Stephen M. Maple, (Alpha Books, 1997).

"Oseola McCarty: A Washerwoman Who Gave All She Had to Help Others, Dies at 91," Rick Bragg, *New York Times,* September 28, 1999.